THE WAY TO GODHOOD

Second text book on the new life that shall lead man from weakness, disease, and death, to freedom from these things, and to strength and power before unknown.

Companion book to "The Way to Life and Immortality."

OUR GOD IS THE GOD OF LIFE, NOT DEATH

Temple of Illuminati

By R. Swinburne Clymer

Printed by
The Philosophical Publishing Co.,
Allentown, Pa.

INTRODUCTORY

Humanity has reached a crisis. That this is true is admitted by all scholars, even by the most conservative We have reached a point that demands a change. Either there must be a step forward or there will be a retrenchment from the plane we now occupy.

That it is possible for us to go backward, to retrograde, is a thing too appalling even to consider, especially when we bear in mind that of the vast multitudes of human beings there are comparatively few who truly live, that comparatively few are masters of their own actions, thinking for themselves, fearing neither orthodox opinions of whatsoever sort nor legislative enactments which might interfere with freedom.

Indeed few men are free. But it must be admitted that there are some who are bound by no creed, no law, no philosophy, except the Great Law of Good. These men would rather do good than to do right. It is possible in some instances for one to do right without doing good, especially in a world and among people where injustice reigns supreme. Men who follow the law of Goodness are masters. It is no small matter to stand alone, and, under all circumstances, to obey the Law of Goodness.

The men of freedom, the men who obey the dictates of goodness, are indeed few in comparison with the vast multitudes who are slaves, slaves in a thousand different ways and to a thousand different things. They are slaves to their own desires and appetites. They desire and secure that which will do them no good, that which works harm and weakness. They have an appetite for those things which bring neither health nor strength. They are slaves to deceptive, negative, destructive teachings, which hold them in bondage and cause them even to fear to think for themselves. They are slaves to beliefs which are founded on superstition, and which give them no freedom of thought. To believe in anything—a creed, a philosophy, or a law—that permits not free thought, is slavery of the worst kind.

But slavery does not end there. Allegiance to any creed, to any philosophy, to any science, so-called, which does not permit freedom of thought also brings with it slavery to personalities, to those who live only for the purpose of exploitation. Being slaves to negative thoughts, desires, appetites, they are an easy prey to the few men and women who live upon the efforts of others. These exploiters of others are men and women of little souls. They are masterful in certain directions. But they are not bound to any moral code; and the Law is not for them. They live as the vampires of the forest live, not by useful labor, but upon the blood, upon the vitality, upon the flesh, of their victims. This is the state of mankind at the present time, at this crisis. Humanity is at the turning of the ways. And, if retrogression should result, both the exploiters and the exploited will go down.

But it is not the fiat of the ages that we should turn back. The New Commandment is given—FORWARD, EVER FORWARD, to greater things, to freedom of being, to MANHOOD, the first indication of Godhood, or supermanhood.

The multitudes have been taught simply *to believe*. They have not been taught *to live, to be, to gain health and strength and power*. Through their beliefs, they have been made slaves, slaves not only to others, but, first of all, to themselves, to their own thoughts, desires and appetites.

Consequently, they are easily enslaved by others in various ways. It is because of ignorance that men are not free. Give man true knowledge, and he will not remain the serf. Give him understanding, and the bondage that holds him will be forced to give way.

It is for this reason that the New Commandment is given to men—that they may gain freedom—freedom from the narrowness of self, first of all; freedom from passion, freedom form fear, freedom from weakness and disease. Greatest of all, freedom from all those things which are brought upon man through belief in negative doctrines, doctrines of weakness, doctrines that inculcate "worm-of-the-dust" principles. There can be no strength where mind is bound by doctrines of this type.

The New Doctrine teaches individual responsibility. It inspires men to be up and doing, to think for themselves and to bear the consequences of their thoughts, and of their acts, without flinching. The man who enters business for himself does so with the intention of trying it, to succeed or to fail, and to bear the consequences of the test. As man enters business with no absolute guarantee of success, so must all men enter life, think for themselves, act according to their instincts and best judgment. Yet must they always remember the one great Law: to think nothing, do nothing, desire nothing, that may bring harm or sorrow, pain or misery, either to themselves or to another. This is the great commandment. It includes all other commandments that men have ever known.

It is, in no wise, the policy of this book to condemn either the poor man or the man of impaired health, or the man of wretchedness and misery. It is the mission of the New Commandment to condemn conditions and environments, negative philosophies and doctrines, which enslave mankind. It is the mission of the New Commandment to point out the way to freedom. Without apology, however, the New Commandment condemns the actions of those who exploit the innocent and the weak and helpless. Nevertheless, it does not indiscriminately condemn wealth and all those who have acquired wealth. For it is to be recognized that wealth may be gained honestly. Wealth that is not gained at the expense of others or through exploitation of the weak and the innocent, is not to be condemned.

Nor is it the mission of the New Commandment to condemn all religion, all philosophies, all science. Far from it, for many of them are teaching constructive doctrines, and are in no wise responsible for the negative doctrines that are reducing the human family to slavery of one kind or another. It is the mission of the New Commandment to teach a doctrine that will, if *lived,* lead man to health, to strength, to possessions that are necessary to happiness, and finally to Immortality and to Sonship with the Father of all.

The New Commandment recognizes that something more than belief and faith is necessary to the true life. It recognizes that faith alone, faith without works, is dead. Faith that does not show its sincerity in works is a false anchorage, which seemingly gives security, a promise of power, but which in reality is a bondage from which few are able to free themselves. The New Commandment demands of mankind more faith, a faith great enough, strong enough, to cause him to *live and to think according to the faith that he professes.*

The New Commandment teaches against mental slavery, against the doctrine of suffering, against the desirability of suffering. It teaches that it is not necessary for man to seek or invite sorrow and suffering in order to reach the goal of Immortality, or Peace Eternal. The New Commandment teaches that man should seek peace of mind, happiness, and innocent pleasures. When suffering does come, we should accept it as men, not in blind faith nor in the necessity of it, but with open mind, with a searching mind. He should seek the cause of suffering, of misery, and of gloom. Then he should seek to remove the cause, since there is no just reason why man should suffer except disobedience of natural and divine law. The New Commandment teaches that pleasures are commendable, and that man should seek for them. If normal and natural, they are not destructive, but are highly constructive and elevating.

Man should go to the child for examples of normal, natural living. The child is natural. It is free from depressing, destructive beliefs and ideas. It accepts pleasure, as they come. It manifests honest, sincere enjoyment of pleasure. Except in those cases in which the child has already learned evil ways from others, it indulges in wholesome activities.

In order to be at his best, in order to reach the highest degree of strength and culture, man must understand certain laws. Among these, and by no means of minor importance, are those laws which have to do with the regulation of daily life. In general, at least, he must accept the three divisions of time—one part of the day for rest, one part of labor, and one part for pleasure, recreation, study, and development of both body and soul. All men, the manual laborer as well as the highest executive, should honor this general division of the day.

The New Commandment makes physical strength and mental well-being of the first importance. Mental strength depends upon physical, while strength of soul depends upon mental vigor, mental health, and mental purity. Moral strength of the highest degree is impossible where there is physical weakness or mental derangement. Consequently, it is of prime importance to understand those laws which have to do with perfect health.

Laws that concern man's well-being physically, mentally, and spiritually cannot, in their highest degree, be enforced by legislative enactments. Only in slight degree, can man be controlled by external laws. Obedience to the laws that pertain to one's highest welfare must be prompted from within one's own being. Mankind must be taught a correct philosophy, a constructive religion, so that they will come to understand that it is *to their own best interests to obey the correct law*. They must obey not because some one else demands it or desires it, not because a law is enforced by state or by an organization, but because their own sense of duty demands it.

The New Commandment holds that a sin against the body is as grievous as a sin against the soul. Whether it be a deliberate act that injures the body or whether it be neglect in caring for the body, it is a violation of the laws of health and strength and efficiency. The soul and the body are equal in importance. One is the temple of God, while the other is potentially the Son of God.

The New Commandment teaches men to seek for happiness in this world, on this plane of being. It is man's heritage to be happy. If he does not find happiness, he is himself at fault; and he fails to find it because of ignorance or disobedience. Man was not placed on earth in order that he should mourn all the days of his life, but that he might experience all conditions and choose those things for life which he finds good and which bring harm to none.

Love is the treasure for which all men seek. Love should be the attracting point in life. For he who finds love finds all else, since life cannot be at its highest without love. Love is of two kinds—love for our fellow men and love for God. Love for our kind on the human plane is the germ, the root, from which love for God springs.

The New Commandment condemns absolutely "love

of ease," a thing that is gradually leading humanity into weakness and decay. Love of ease is nothing else than sluggishness of life. It is spiritual beggarism. The healthy, strong human being, in whom there is a living spark of divinity, desires to be a creator. He desires to labor, to accomplish; and love of ease in man is a positive sign of decay.

The New Commandment teaches that labor is honorable. Labor of some worthy, constructive kind is necessary for all, the rich as well as the poor; and whoever does not perform some useful labor gradually falls into decay, and brings about his own destruction. Those nations in the past who followed pastoral occupations, where labor in the fields and the woods was necessary, were the strongest, the healthiest, the happiest, and the most Godlike people of the world. Labor is necessary to all men, no matter what their station in life, if they would be normal and natural and healthy and strong, both physically and mentally, and if they would be more like God, their Creator.

The New Commandment, based on Manhood leading to Godhood, is a religion that is *life itself*. It is a religion of the heart and the mind, of the soul and the body. It is a religion that includes the whole being. It is a holy religion. Nor is it worship of Nature in any sense of the word. It glorifies Nature, however. It glorifies humanity, in order that the Soul of Man, the Son of God, and God himself, may be glorified therein.

The New Commandment teaches freedom, and commands all men to seek for liberty, but liberty that is of the self and not at the expense of one's fellow creature.

Fraternally,

THE AUTHOR.

"Beverly," January 13th, 1914.

CHAPTER ONE

MANHOOD AND RESPONSIBILITY, THE GOAL.

For long centuries, negativeness had been the rule among mankind. True, it is freely admitted that during these centuries there have been a few men who have ruled with an iron hand. These were positive in the extreme. But the vast multitudes under these men were practically slaves; for theirs was the duty to obey the slightest wish of those in power. They held no thought contrary to the thoughts of the ruler. If the ruler said war, all were ready to obey the call. If he said work, all were ready for work.

This is negativeness. There is no individual responsibility attached to such a life. The life is ruled by others, and on them falls the actual responsibility.

How ignoble is the life that is ruled by another mind! How ignoble, the life that is controlled by another in all its actions, aye, even in its thoughts! The acts committed by those who are mere slaves to the behests of another bring with them a certain train of thought, even a certain religious belief; and, eventually, the one so controlled by another has lost all sense of responsibility, even in the exercise of judgment.

But the spirit of the long ago is fast passing away—the spirit of supreme negativeness. The new age has begun, the age of activity and positiveness. In the new age, gradually, though it may be slowly, men will, first of all, begin to think for themselves. More than this, they will not shrink from the responsibility of acting according to their thought. This will make of man an individual, it will give him manhood.

Throughout the centuries, it has been generally accepted, that, if an individual obeys the laws of the land and if he gives a reasonable support to the religious form that receives the sanction of the ruling power, he thereby meets the conditions of being a man. But that idea is dead and gone. No longer is an individual thought of as a man simply because he is of the male sex.

To be a man in the true sense demands that he must think and act for himself. He must have the courage of his own convictions. To do this and that, simply for the sake of winning the approval of some friend or some one in authority, to act thus and so simply because some one in power advocates it, does not meet the conditions of manhood and individual responsibility.

The way to manhood is the way to power. But it must be understood that the way to manhood and power is the way of individual responsibility. But with responsibility comes the strength to be responsible, the strength to carry and to shoulder greater responsibility. This brings out individuality in man. It develops manhood. And he who reaches manhood's true estate is well on the way to Godhood.

The new doctrine, the coming science-religion-philosophy, is the only law a strong man needs. Unless he is a weakling, he does not need external laws to force him to do thus and so. The new doctrine does not lay down definite rules of action. It is a system of life. It teaches man so to think, so to live, so to act, as to bring out the potential power in himself, thereby developing latent manhood. Through accepting the responsibility that rests upon him, he gains more and more strength, his manhood becomes more and more reliable, and he is led on and on toward Godhood.

Man cannot solve the problem of existence by ignoring the duties of life, by holding himself in a negative state, by taking everything for granted, by looking upon life as an evil in itself, or by accepting things as they come, whether good or not good, with no effort to improve them.

The new doctrine proposes that man must take up the duties of life actively and positively. He must carefully consider all calls that are made upon him. He must hold himself in an active, positive state, but with no antagonism toward anything whatever, never with hate or malice toward any person or any condition. He must ever defend the right, the true self, defending it actively and positively, but with no malice or hatred or animosity, with no censure or harsh judgment, or ill-will, with no grudge or bitterness or envy. This—to be free from antagonism and censue of every type and description—is a prime essential of the positive type of mind which is unreservedly advocated by the New Commandment.

The New Commandment teaches man to look upon life as good. Existence in the present state is desirable, and is a positive and absolute good. Life on the present plane is not only necessary, but even glorious. If man accepts it as such, and considers every duty a pleasure, and if he does everything with the thought that it is for the best—by this attitude of mind, he shows himself a man in the true sense of the word. By persisting in this attitude of mind and by executing the duties of life in this spirit, he shows himself more than a man. By executing the duties of life in this wholesome positive spirit, he manifests the possibility of attaining Godhood.

Life is not an evil, nor are the acts of the true life an evil. Nor are the pleasures of life an evil. They become evil only when indulgence in them results in harm either to the self or to another. Not otherwise are they evil. All things that come to man are for a purpose. By denying them or by accounting them evil, we accomplish nothing. Neither do we accomplish anything, on the other hand, by meekly accepting all things as something to be accepted or as necessary evils to be endured. To accept things thus makes of man nothing more nor less than a mere negative machine, a nothingness.

Things which come to us in life are either to be accepted and acted on or they are to be cast aside as unworthy of our acceptance and unworthy of our performance. We are to give them careful consideration in order to determine whether they represent the positive or the negative side of life. If the negative, we should reject them or extract the positive aspects from the negative and encourage only the positive features.

It matters not whether some one wishes to force certain conditions upon us, this is no excuse for our accepting them. Whether they come before us in the guise of duty or whether some one apparently stronger than we ourselves wants to press them upon us, the New Commandment teaches that the mode of procedure is the same in so far as we are concerned. We are to consider the matter thoroughly, and carefully weigh conditions to determine whether they are for the good of ourselves and of others. If careful weighing of conditions proves that there is an advantage in accepting, then it is our duty to do so, even though we may not want to. For, in refusing, we refuse our duty and thereby become more negative, more the slave to conditions, more in the coils of the destructive serpent.

If, however, investigation shows that the proffered conditions are detrimental in that they may weaken us or bring disadvantage or bring advantage attended by injury to ourselves or others, then it is our duty to refuse them. The New Commandment demands that we shall refuse them even though great power and great influence are brought to bear to force us to do otherwise.

The New Commandment, "Be a Man that thou mayst become a god," insists that each individual is a free agent, and that no one can offer the excuse that he is forced to do thus and so.

Under no consideration is life to be accounted evil. It never has been evil and never will be, unless the one who lives it makes it so of his own free choice. Through the experiences of life, either we become men and women, individuals, beings gradually tending, by means of our own manhood and womanhood, toward Godhood.

To the soul, life is a kindergarten. Through existence in the present state and on the present plane, we gain experience. It is here that we learn our lessons. It is here that we are tested, as the ore is tested in the furnace, only with the difference that the ore has no power of choice and must give up its gold; whereas, man, through the power of free-will, may refuse to liberate the gold. The ore accepts the conditions of the furnace and sets free its gold. It is possible for man to accept conditions as a helpless slave, and, even though he may suffer severely under the heat of the testing, he may refuse to learn the lesson and refuse to appropriate its blessings. With man, something more than mere acceptance of conditions is necessary. He must accept in the right spirit. He must learn through the experience, and obey. He must let go of the dross, and love the gold into expression. This is the positive attitude of mind. This manifests manhood and a responsible attitude toward life's conditions.

Life, as we know it, is necessary for the soul and also necessary for the body. Without life on this plane, the soul could not become individualized, could not gain experience, could not become like the gods. The growth that results from wise experience can come only through being positive at all times, the master of self, the slave of none, choosing the things that are an advantage and refusing the things that are a disadvantage.

The positive attitude of mind requires courage. But, as in all things else, courage grows through deliberate choice, on the one hand, through deliberate refusal, on the other. With courage comes strength, and with strength comes greater power to do and to accomplish.

The individual who accepts all things as they come, with no effort to master or to improve them is a negative life. The negative life is always the weak, diseased, unfruitful life. Through negativeness comes pessimism. Pessimism is like the water standing in the pool that has no outlet. It becomes a deadly poison. Such a poison and malaria-breeding condition is pessimism in the heart of man. There is strength and power in every individual, though it may be in an inert state. He who accepts all things as they come, thinking them to be evils which must be endured, is like the stagnant pool of water. He never uses his powers and his capabilities. He fails to become strong; for he gives no opportunity to the Man within, the god in embryo, to assert himself. As a result, his life becomes stagnant and eventually dies out, as the pool of water dries up and loses its individuality.

The New Commandment teaches the doctrine of manhood, of strength, of self-government. The individual who accepts the spirit of the command, "Be a man and thou mayst be a god," needs not to be governed by laws, by governments, by armies. He sees the glory and the beauty of life, and is too much of an entity, too much of a man, to do that which may harm either himself or others. To him, life is glorious. He recognizes that life here is the means to a greater life, and that every act performed with full sanction of the reason for it will make the doer stronger and more of a man, and therefore nearer to Godhood.

To such an individual, may come the time when demands will be made upon him to do those things which do not fit into the true life and which do not receive the sanction of the command to be a man in order that one may become a god. These demands may come from those who are near and dear to him. But, if he realizes that the things demanded of him do not coincide with the Higher Ideal to which he has consecrated his life, he must summon all courage and strength to withstand their entreaties. He must assert his individuality, and call upon all the forces of his being, in order to obey the dictates of his enlightened conscience.

His refusal to comply with the wishes of his loved ones, may give rise to many conditions hard to meet, conditions unforeseen and unbelievable, even to the most vivid imagination. But, no matter what the result or the outcome, to him, it is always the same. He will face the crisis with firmness and with courage. He will not go counter to, or compromise, his convictions of right. Nevertheless,—and note well this point—the New Commandment, "Be a Man," demands that, in it all and through it all, he shall entertain no censure, no malice, no ill-will, no antagonism, no bitterness, towards those who are instrumental in placing him in such a crisis. The New Commandment, which exacts of every individual manhood, honor, and a sense of responsibility, as well as a prophetic recognition of Godhood, is also exacting in its demands that, in it all and through it all, he shall be free from resentment and harsh judgment toward · conditions as well as personalities.

This is the meaning of a positive state of mind as opposed to a negative. Not only is the positive mind firm in the position that it deliberately takes, but it is also free from antagonism toward those who are the instruments of testing its strength. Not only does it fight to the bitter end for its best understanding of right, but it also preserves equanimity of spirit and a rigid control over itself, allowing no personal grudge or malice to gain entrance into the sacred precincts over which the New Commandment is establishing its power.

It is not an impossibility for one to give his life rather than to forfeit allegiance to the Ideal Standard he has placed before himself. But, by losing his life in the contest of right, he only gains a greater life. While he who yields to carnal authority when divine authority bids him Nay, becomes slave to carnal forces. In this way, he sells his birthright, and enters serfdom to those who have forced him to violate the command to be a Man and thereby eventually to become a god.

The New Commandment, with all its pronounced emphasis upon firmness, and positiveness as opposed to negativeness and destruction, by no means advocates antagonism to establish authority. On the contrary, obedience thereto, in so far as it is possible, is clearly and unmistakably encouraged. Strict obedience to the Law of Right and of Goodness, above all else, it teaches. Refusal to comply with the wish of friend and enemy alike is demanded when compliance means to degrade the Divine Spark, which is indeed both "author and finisher" of the command, "Be a Man and thou mayst be a god."

The doctrine of manhood and responsibility teaches not nihilism. It teaches absolute individuality. It does not teach a return to nothingness, as the goal and as the only satisfactory outcome of the bane and the evil of existence. On the contrary, it teaches a return to Godhood, as the goal and as the natural and inevitable outcome of living the life that exalts manhood and develops the Godhood latent in man. As the natural outcome of the beauty and the glory of existence, it anticipates Individualized God Consciousness—this, the goal, far from nihilism and loss of identity in the Great Sea of Universal Substance!

In the life of those who accept the New Commandment as their standard, hate and other forms of destructive ness can have no place, for the reason that hate and kindred forms of destructiveness can accomplish nothing. No matter what demands may be made upon one, no matter how unreasonable or unjust, to hate those who press hard and cruel conditions upon him and to feel malice toward them, does not add strength to resist the demands and to surmount the obstacles placed in his way. This one point is the foundation argument—the basic reason—for not giving way to negative and destructive states of mind. Whereas—to repeat by stating the same thought affirmatively—by holding one's mind positively and actively free from hate and ill-will toward the agents of undesirable measures, he gains marvellous strength and power, which may be used in resisting the demands and in surmounting the obstacles placed in his way. Hate and malice, being in themselves negative and evil, ally the soul in which they are held with the very forces that demand unreasonable things of him, and thereby he is weakened.

The true spirit of resistance is simply to consider the demands as wrong and not to comply, and yet to recognize that those who make the demand have not yet learned the Law, and therefore are not to be judged harshly for their point of view. The true spirit of resistance is firm in its refusal, but it is equally firm in maintaining the positive attitude of kindness and non-censure toward all parties involved.

Thus it is seen that hate and malice are never called for, and that good never comes from them. A summing up of all the strength of the being is necessary for emergencies. A love power that recognizes the good of existence and the right of choice, a love power that also gives to others the right of choice, the right to live their lives according to their standard—this is a requisite of the command, "Be a Man and thou mayst be a god." Firmness with one's self is demanded, not only the firmness that holds one true to one's own standard of right, but the firmness that refuses to interfere, even in thought and feeling, with the liberty of others. This is the attitude of mind that brings power; and, though temporary suffering may come from it, such suffering actually brings greater power and greater manhood, and allies one more closely with the Godhead.

Furthermore, it must be remembered that to comply with an unjust demand may, for the time being, give freedom. But it is quite possible that this freedom and the consequent compliance with an unjust request may put the one granting it in a bondage extending through ages, and may even end in complete destruction of that which should have become, first of all, an individual, a Man, and, lastly, a god. For be it remembered that Godhood can never be reached except by the way of manhood and individuality.

In life, there are but two paths. The one is the path of negativeness and pessimism. It grows out of the belief that existence itself is evil and undesirable, and that the only way to become free from it is to comply with every request and every urge, and to offer no resistance whatever to them, no matter what their nature. It grows out of the mistaken notion that a machine-like acceptance of all conditions, a resignation that questions not, a submission that meekly acquiesces and patiently endures, ends eventually in a state of glory. According to the new doctrine, rather than leading to a state of glory, it leads to destruction and annihilation. For negativeness in itself is a state of destruction, because, through negativeness, everything in the system is poisoned, and even the good that might be therein, like the water in the stagnant pool, is become a poison. This state of being ends in nihilism; for it is the negative, nihilistic state. There is no strength, manhood is missing; and, where manhood is missing, Godhood cannot be found.

The other path is the path of positiveness and otpimism. Let there be no misconception regarding the words, positive and positiveness. Let it be emphasized that they do not refer to the state of mind that thinks itself alone in the right, nor do they refer to a pompous stubbornness nor to a disagreeable aggressiveness in pushing one's own claim or one's own views. These words refer to the attitude of mind that looks upon life and existence on this plane as beneficent in its purposes and in its possibilities. The positive attitude examines all things with open mind and heart, and calmly rejects that which savors of destructiveness. It determines its acts by whether they promise to be of advantage followed by no disadvantage, by whether they promise good results attended by no detrimental effects. More than this, the positive attitude refuses to harbour destructive thought and feeling toward any person or condition. This is one of the most truly essential conditions of true positiveness. It is apt to be overlooked as a requisite of the positive attitude. That love and goodness and kindness in judgment of others, and generosity of spirit toward both men and things, are active, positive, strong, virile virtues, is a truth that needs pronounced and unsparing emphasis. These are the essentials of strength and manhood and honor. The day is past when brutality and cruelty and domineering aggressiveness are to be associated with the positive attitude of mind. Ever and always is the positive attitude optimistic and hopeful; for it is based on the law of constructiveness and growth.

This is the path that leads to manhood. In every unworthy impulse resisted, there is increased strength. The personality becomes the individuality, and eventually the individuality rises to Godhood.

The disappointments of life cannot be avoided by shunning the responsibilities of life. The life that undertakes to shun disappointments is a continual disappointment in itself. It is a life that is fundamentally negative. It is a reed-like life, which is blown this way and that by every gust of wind, by every opinion, never at peace with itself or with the work in which it is engaged, never finding happiness, but ever meeting disappointments and misery, full of censure and bitterness because conditions are not as the negative mind thinks they should be.

Such a life, though lived under the belief that it is honoring God, is, nevertheless, tending continually toward nihilism so long as it holds the negative point-of-view toward all things. With nihilism, there is neither responsibility nor reward, neither love nor hate. With nihilism, there is nothing except a long dream of nothingness, from which there is no awakening; for the latent power of the individual has passed on to the great chasm of nothingness, there to be reformed, it may be, and, possibly, to be made use of by another entity. The old being has passed away, it has been changed, not by the individual, but by the power of the Great Law, which either forces us to bring out all latent possibilities within us or does it for us. Note this point, however; when the Law does it for us, it takes the right cf individuality from us, and another being is given the opportunity of developing into individuality the Divine Spark that had been ours. This is the price, the reward, of nihilism.

Life itself is a responsibility. The sooner mankind comes to a recognition of this fact, the better it will be. The sooner this fact is understood, the sooner will a true, natural, divine, beautiful state of existence on this plane be brought about, wherein all will accept life as worthy and desirable. Responsibility is the way to manhood. Manhood is the way to Godhood and deific power and deific conciousness.

CHAPTER TWO

HEAVEN, THE STATE OF HAPPINESS, MUST BE FOUND ON EARTH.

Prevalent among all former schools of religion and philosophy has been the belief that earthly happiness is a dream, an impossibility, and that, even if it were possible for man to know happiness on earth, it would be a mortal sin to seek happiness. Contrary to this doctrine, the New Commandment teaches, absolutely and without qualification, that earthly happiness is a possibility, nay, even more, that it is a necessity, since those who do not find peace and happiness on this plane will not find it on any other plane of being, that for them peace and happiness do not exist.

There may be, however, different standards in regard to what constitutes peace and happiness. If the one criterion of happiness is earthly possessions and carnal sense-delights, then, the New Commandment agrees with the prevalent teaching that it is a snare and a delusion, a phantom of mortal mind, a chimera, even an impossibility. The New Commandment holds the standard that peace and happiness come through living in harmony with the laws of God and of Nature. When man lives in harmony with Nature and his God, the mind finds peace and the conscience gives rest. The two—a peaceful mind and a restful conscience—constitutes true happiness. This type of happiness is independent of, and superior to, earthly possessions.

Happiness is a factor to which all men have right. In other words, all men can find happiness if they seek for it according to the laws of true happiness. Peace and happiness are as natural to the true human being as are eating ar.d sleeping; in fact, they form a part of his life, as do eating and sleeping. So interrelated, indeed, are happiness and the ordinary functions of life that one can not be thoroughly happy if normal functioning of physical organs is interfered with. Happiness depends in part upon good health.

Good health, nevertheless, which is simply the result of a natural life, is not the only means to happiness and peace. Even with good health, one cannot be entirely contented and at peace, unless he possesses a conscience that is free from accusation and a mind that follows the path toward freedom.

The slave, bound to a master, whether that master be the church, the state, some other agency, or his own "selfish self," is not free. He can become free only by asserting the power of the inner Man and by exacting of himself obedience to the law of his own divine nature. The man that is afraid to think for himself, afraid to do what he thinks is right, afraid to assert himself, knows not happiness and peace. The path of freedom is the path to happiness.

The New Commandment exalts manhood and womanhood, and insists that, to become a complete being and to exemplify the divine attributes latent in him, was the one aim and design of the Father in sending forth His soul-children to this plane in bodies of flesh. It is here they gain experience. Here they choose whether to be of free mind or whether to be in bondage. No man has greater right to his ideals than has another. The right to ideas is not dependent upon external authority nor upon social distinction, but upon degree of wisdom and knowledge.

Ignorance is a hard and a most cruel taskmaster. There can be no freedom so long as man hugs to his breast ignorance and an "all-wise" opinion. He who refuses to read and to study, who refuses to be a learner of

God and Nature, is a slave to ignorance and his own petty whims—a slave, iron-bound and shackled.

In knowledge and wisdom, gained through experience and study and application, in the proper use of knowledge and wisdom—in these alone, is to be found health, freedom, peace, and happiness. These, without exception, must be found by man here and now; for, in the life beyond, bereft of a physical body, man cannot find them.

Happiness is the birthright of man. If he does not find it, whose fault is it? All the laws of Nature proclaim that happiness is the heritage of man. The birds, though they may be killed the next moment, sing songs of joy, caring nothing for a future day or year, but living in the *Now,* happy, joyful, tuneful, because they live according to their nature, obeying the laws of their being, abusing no faculty, and being in bondage to no one in the bird kingdom.

Man has the same right and the same privilege. As the bird lives in the bird world, absolutely healthful because it obeys the laws of its kingdom, so man may live in the human kingdom, strong, vigorous, and healthful because he is obedient to the laws of his kingdom. As the bird forgets the past and thinks not of the future, and sings a song of happiness in the present, so may man in his world learn from the bird, wisdom, trust, and peace. The bird is wise in the wisdom of its kingdom, while man is ignorant in respect to himself and his plane of being; and, through ignorance, he becomes the slave both to himself and to others. Strange to say, a false philosophy and religion have made him believe that happiness is an error, a mortal sin, a something not intended for man in this world, something, which, however, he may gain in the next world as a reward for denying himself happiness in this life. Such a religion forgets that, in all things, man must make a beginning, and that this world is *the world*

of beginnings, and that it may also be the world of end-
ings, provided the beginning is made here and now.

An error, indeed, is it to believe that the desire for
earthly happiness is a chimera that lures man on to destruction, and leads him on to error and sin, and that, if
continually held, will force the soul of man to return to
earth again and again until it is free from the desire. The
desire for happiness is simply the desire for peace and
perfection. No man can be fully perfect until he is entirely happy. Nor can one reach entire happiness until
he has reached perfection. The desire for happiness is
not an error or a sin. Yet equally true is it that the desire for happiness grows and changes, expands and modi-
fies itself, as man advances toward perfection. Ultimate
happiness and ultimate perfection are identical.

Perfection demands freedom, freedom from disease,
from ignorance, and from every kind of bondage. Likewise, happiness demands freedom, freedom from disease,
sin, and bondage to this and that, bondage to beliefs in this
or that, bondage to opinions because others hold them,
bondage to conditions because one is too inert or too negative to cast off the shackles that bind—this is the antith-
esis of happiness. Happiness ever means freedom, freedom from an accusing conscience, freedom from the bondage that binds to dogmatic opinions. Happiness comes in
proportion as one gains freedom.

When man realizes that he is strong enough to stand
alone, no matter if all the world is against him, strong
enough to bear what is placed upon him, even though it
shall swing his body into Eternity, then has he attained a
good degree of freedom and self-reliance, then has he attained a good degree of peace and happiness. For he well
knows that, to stand thus, frees his soul from bondage so
that he can face the Eternal Judge with a smile. The
Judge of all, seeing him free from mankind and their

earthly passions, will be only too glad to honor him who has dared to be strong, dared to be a Man and to reach Godhood.

The desire for happiness is a natural desire. It is, moreover, a spiritual desire, a desire of the soul. Without this desire, man would not seek to raise himself from the earth-level, but would be content to live as the beast of the field. Practically universal, however, is it among mankind to desire some type of happiness. More than this, practically universal is it to desire knowledge with happiness—knowledge as to why man is, and why he is to continue to be.

In desire, we do not find sin and destruction; but we find therein the first incentive to something better. True desire may take an abnormal course, seeking for that which leads to destruction. This, however, is not the fault of that in man which we call desire, rather is it the fault of the man himself; for he is not a free man, but a slave to those things which destroy.

It is the desire that causes man to seek for wisdom. Desire for wisdom is really desire for happiness. There must be a reason for desiring wisdom. Surely man does not seek wisdom for the sake of pain and sorrow. Seldom, indeed, does he seek it for destruction or for ignoble purposes. He seeks wisdom because he longs to be free from bondage, the bondage of ignorance and unjust judgment, the bondage of disease and error, the bondage that binds him to others. Freedom from bondage, such as this, means happiness and peace to him, not only in another world, but even in the Here and the Now.

Twin sister to the desire for happiness is the desire for pleasure. Every normal soul desires the innocent pleasures of life. It is an error to consider all pleasure as sinful and as belonging to the evil one. Like all things else, pleasures are of two classes, according to the use made of them. Those are good, which bring harm to no one. Those are evil, which bring pain and suffering, sorrow and disappointment, either to the one indulging in them or to others.

Pleasure in itself and of itself is not evil. Man has been given the faculty of enjoyment because it is right for him to enjoy. He has been given the opportunity so to live, so to act, that pleasures shall be a part of life. For this very reason, it is right for him to enjoy. For, in order to enjoy, he must pay the price of enjoyment. To pay the price entitles him to the right of enjoyment.

The fact that man is endowed with a certain possibility or faculty is in itself proof that he should make use of it. The mere fact that he can be happy, that he can enjoy, indicates that he should seek happiness and enjoyment. He should, indeed, make every effort to find peace and happiness, joy and contentment; for these, normally gratified, are a part of man's true nature.

The goal of peace, the sublime ending of life, can never be obtained through destroying or obliterating the desire for pleasure. In truth, he who tries to avoid peace and happiness, even under a mistaken notion that earthly joy is forbidden man, becomes through that very view of life, an inert machine, a something ungodly and unholy, a creature that does nothing useful in life, that makes no effort to help his fellow man, that performs no useful labor, a non-entity, which deserves to be shunned by all normal beings. On the other hand, he who does a good deed to a poor soul finds within himself a sense of well-doing, a feeling of peace. This is happiness in a degree. If this is to be avoided, then, the little deeds of kindness are to be avoided.

No matter what our deed may be, if it is something that will help an unfortunate creature, we cannot help feeling that we have done well. In fact, the pleasure and the gladness that we see upon the face and in the eye of him whom we favor causes us to feel a like state of happiness; and this, instead of being an evil, is as food for the soul, is to the soul what bread is to the body.

Let us go out in the sunshine on a spring day and see the sun in its springtime glory. The flowers in the tree, the birds in the air—all nature, in fact, is wearing a smile of gladness. The air is fresh, balmy, and exhilarating. If we succeed in forgetting the self for a time, we too may be as happy as Nature herself. This, again, is an indication of what man may be if he is willing to come into harmony with the laws of God and Nature. For God is the ruler of Nature, and Nature is always happy, so are all things that obey Nature's laws.

Let us seek happiness. But let us not seek to find it at the expense of any living creature. Rather, let us seek it through the help we can give to God's creatures. Every smile won from God's creatures, every smile won from God's children, will send a ray of happiness to your own heart and soul, and will add to the store of happiness that is becoming part of it.

He who refuses to seek earthly happiness, and sits with gloom on his face and darkness in his heart, refusing the instruction offered him by Nature simply because he thinks that, through happiness here, he forfeits the right to happiness in the Beyond, is entirely selfish, more selfish than the beggar that steals bread from the hungry child, allowing the child to go hungry. The beggar may do good deeds and partly atone for his wrongs; but he who sits in gloom, refusing all chances of obtaining happiness and peace, is an alien from God and a stranger to his fellow man.

It may seem strange to claim that he who seeks not happiness is selfish. But, when it is remembered that happiness comes only through making others happy, it is clearly seen how utterly selfish and ignoble is he who shuns earthly happiness. Manhood is not "part and parcel" of such a life. And where manhood is not, Godhood is not.

Happiness, in its highest degree, is found in forgetting the self. Forgetfulness of self cannot be attained while we fear to do this or that because it may harm us in some way; for that very fear is self-condemnatory in that it admits weakness within. He knows not happiness with whom the ghost of fear is ever present, his close companion by day and by night.

But the man who, through careful thought and study, gradually grows into the state of fearing nothing except the lashing of his own conscience; the man who will stand firm, and even stand alone, regardless of the opinions of others—he is the man that shall gradually free himself from the ghost of fear and from the bondage of dogma and unnatural laws. By so doing, he becomes a Man, an individual, eventually, a god. He knows peace and happiness, even though he were burned at the stake; for freedom is within. Peace and contentment are within. And within is the matchless knowledge that he is free, free as the gods, free as the birds of the air, free and glorious as the lily that blooms in the field.

These are the true freedmen. These are the gods, who, though on earth, are, nevertheless, not of the earth. These are the men who find happiness on earth. They can be no happier in a heaven than they are on the earth. Earth does not end where heaven begins, nor does heaven begin where earth ends. But heaven is here and now. Heaven begins on earth. It is to be found in the heart of the man that has gained his freedom, not because he has asked for it, but because he has *demanded* it, because he was Man enough to uphold his demands in spite of all that may have been done or said to prevent him from obtaining freedom of heart, of mind, of soul, and of body.

CHAPTER THREE

Life, Not a Disease, an Evil, from Which to Fight for Freedom.

In itself, life is good; and in life all good things may be found. Even Immortality must be found while in the earth life; and, unless it is found while the soul dwells in the flesh, it will never be found.

The body was given to the soul and the spirit so that the soul might manifest through the body. The body of man is like the earth, like the ground, in which is planted a seed. Under favorable conditions, the seed will spring up and bear fruit. We may well call the fruit of the plant the resurrection, or the Illumination, of the plant.

In like manner, the Divine Spark, the embryonic soul, is placed in the body of man. Under favorable conditions, the body is to the soul what the earth is to the seed. The soul will germinate and grow, becoming strong and comely, gradually reaching the state of consciousness that we call Illumination; and, through Illumination, man becomes one of the gods.

All this would be utterly impossible, were it not for the earth life and the earth body. Consequently, life on earth and earth existence is not an evil, but a potential good, a thing that is intrinsically desirable, a thing to be sought for. But, just in proportion as the life is constructive and positive, in proportion as the thoughts are normal and uplifting, in that proportion will the blessings of Nature and of God be showered upon man.

Considering the matter in this light, we find that earthly blessings are not curses, which drag down the soul, not curses, which prevent man from reaching the other kingdom, called heaven, when he passes from the earth life to the soul world. Rather are earthly blessings to be thought of as the beginning of that life in the soul realm, upon which man enters when he is freed from the body.

Even earthly blessings come to no man unless he has earned them, unless he has become worthy of them. Teachings to the contrary, whether they are of science, religion, or philosophy, are negative and destructive, and spring from a mind that is diseased and distorted, disordered and unnatural.

Rather than being undesirable, and something to be shunned, something from which we are to free ourselves as soon as possible, the earth life is a thing to hold on to and to be prolonged as much as possible. The longer the earth life can be prolonged, the more opportunity man has to free himself from all those things which are undesirable in his nature and in his environment, things from which he must free himself sooner or later; and, in order to attain freedom from these difficulties of character and environment, he must return to the earth life again and again, until he has fully gained freedom.

It is undeniable that there are many things in life which are not desirable, things which require patience and even suffering in overcoming them. But the earth life is a school in which we are taught valuable lessons and gain valuable experiences and training. If we are wise, and learn our lessons well, and gain skill in self-mastery from the trining offered, if we are careful not to repeat mistakes, thereby being forced to relearn lessons, we will fully realize that life is indeed a blessing, and, even through sorrow and misfortune, we may gain lasting advantage and eternal benefit,

On the other hand, it is equally true that, if man is rebellious in disposition or cowardly at heart, if he is not willing to obey the laws of Nature, which, at times, demand that we shall deny ourselves temporary happiness for the sake of permanent good, we shall be made to suffer; and, that which was apparently a blessing becomes a punishment. This, however, is not due to the fact that life in itself is a curse. It is due to the fact that we have chosen unwisely and have not yet learned that manhood dwells potentially within each one.

In ancient Pompeii, it was the custom for slaves to wear a scarf or a belt, which marked them as slaves. If, in modern times, all who are slaves either to themeslves and their unnatural appetites and desires or to some creed or belief or power, were to wear such a belt or scarf, we would see few men without the scarf of serfdom. For this reason—because all, or nearly all, are slaves of some one or some thing, and have not manhood enough to free themselves from their own peculiar type of personal bondage—we hear the cry that life is undesirable, and an evil to be endured until the time is ripe to become free from it. Those who raise this cry are thereby branding themselves as slaves, as surely as if they wore the scarf of serfdom. They have yet to learn their own potential power. They have yet to realize that they are freeborn, that theirs is the power of manhood, and that manhood leads to Godhood, and to freedom, and to all things which are desired by man.

The wise man knows that there are times when self-denial is not only a virtue, but even a power-producer. At these times, he denies the desires and the appetites in order that he may become stronger and more of a man, also in order that he may avoid the punishment that invariably results when the laws that concern true manhood are broken.

To become wise, to obtain the fruits of wisdom, demands a study of the laws of nature and the laws of being. These laws are really identical, but are different in their application.

Thus, in order to be truly man, in order to have the greatest amount of strength and power, it is necessary that one should so live as to be as free as possible from disease and physical weakness.

The ignorant one, he who exults in self-wisdom, will smile at the idea that food and drink and daily habits of life have anything to do with happiness and eternal welfare. He indulges in everything, good and bad, and reaps the reward of his ignorance and his arrogance; and, being disease-racked and in misery, he curses life on this plane, and tries to free himself from it, thinking that, by so doing, he is honoring God and preparing himself for a happier state in another sphere. In fact, he is doing nothing of the kind, but is suffering because of his ignorance, and knows no more of God than he knows of true manhood. His religion is pessimistic. Those things which the healthy, normal man enjoys and finds happiness in, look evil to him; and he condemns them, and would delegate all those who follow them to a sphere called Hades—a place that, to healthy-minded folk, has no existence.

It is from abnormal brains, which are under the rule of an abused body, that we receive the many pessimistic philosophies—philosophies, in which there is nothing but condemnation of all that is good and true, of all that is glorious in life. Originators of pessimistic philosophies are themselves slaves to misery, and, consequently, must preach a doctrine of inharmony. When denial has to do with things that bring harm to any part of the four-fold being or to others, it is praiseworthy, and brings greater power, greater peace, and greater happiness. But, when self-denial becomes abnormal, it degrades, tears down Manhood, destroys the peace and the happiness of others, and steeps the self in misery.

Twin-sister to an abnormal self-denial, but far more evil and destructive, is self-abhorrence—that destructive doctrine which teaches man that he is a worm of the dust, that he should torture and abuse the physical being, and welcome pain and disease and misery in order that the soul may become a bright angel in the next world. Than this, no doctrine could be more far-reaching in its destructive effects. It has held vast multitudes for centuries. The western nations, however, are freeing themselves from it, and are gradually accepting the New Commandment— the doctrine that, in true and noble manhood alone, are honor and glory to be ascribed to the Father of all. But, in the East, self-torture, the result of the doctrine of self-abhorrence, is still too much in power among the people. There, the belief is still prevalent that, through self-torture, the soul becomes great and glorious. Whereas, in reality, man ignores God and His laws, and degrades Him more in no other way than by degrading the self.

Man is created in the image of God. Within him dwells a Divine Spark, part of the Father. In no other way can he glorify God more than by perfecting the Divine Spark, Image of the Father, by bringing into manifestation every power possessed by the normal body. This cannot be accomplished by denying the body the things that are natural and normal, nor can it be accomplished through self-abhorrence. Abnormal self-denial and self-abhorrence will stultify the body and bring it weakness and disease and suffering, which is contrary to Nature, to Reason, and to God.

The New Commandment is strict in its demands that man shall become truly a Man, that he shall glorify God by glorifying himself. In no other way can he do this bet-

ter than by living the normal life, as man should live.
This will give strength and beauty to the whole being. In
particular, it will give strength and power and beauty to
the Soul, Image of the Divine.

No longer is it regarded by the enlightened mind that
self-abhorrence is a virtue, but, rather, that it is a disgrace,
a weakness, slavery to a dogma with no foundation of
truth. Life based on such a dogma leads to weakness, to
sorrow, to suffering, and, in the end, to loss of the individuality of the Divine Spark, which might have become a
living, illuminated Soul, an honor to God, the Father.

The New Commandment teaches man not to seek for
sorrow and suffering. He will have his full share without
seeking for it. Almost universally, men are living in ignorance; and, though they may be of open mind, before
they can learn wisdom and the way of a natural life, they
are sure to suffer. As a rule, man is not willing to learn
from the experiences of others. He is inclined to think
that he is different from his fellow man, and that he will,
in some way, escape the disastrous consequences of his
own deeds. Unquestionably, God honors the man that
bears suffering in silence and without complaint when suffering has become necessary because of ignorant or wilful
breaking of natural law. But it must be a reproach to
God to see man seeking for means whereby he may bring
suffering upon himself under the mistaken idea that it
pleases God to see His children suffer.

The New Commandment teaches a full life. It
teaches ways and means to avoid suffering, sorrow, and
misery, ways and means by which to free himself from
sin and sickness. It teaches him how to attain perfection of body, peace of mind, and Illumination of Soul. It
teaches, absolutely and without exception, that Manhood
is the first requisite to Godhood, and that perfection of
body, peace of mind, and Illumination of Soul lead to Immortality and to conscious Sonship with the Father.

The work of man on earth is twofold, and he owes a twofold duty, each of which is always interwoven with the other.

One duty is to the soul, the spiritual self, and to the Father, of which it is a part. The other duty is to the body and to Mother Earth, or Nature. He must do his duty to both, in order to be a full, complete Man.

He must do nothing that will cause him to tire of life and the happiness that life gives to man. Body and soul are equal in importance. Each requires special effort to perfect. But the life of man may be so ordered as to perfect both of them at the same time. But this can never be accomplished by considering that the body and its normal demands are unnatural and to be ignored. Rather, this is to be accomplished by recognizing the fact that the body has needs which must be supplied, and by making conscious efforts to bring the body to the highest state of perfection and freedom from all things that are not desirable. By so doing, he helps the Soul within the body; for the things that harm the body will also harm the soul, since the two are closely interwoven, and one is not independent of the other.

In order to be perfect, man must seek the things in the earth life that bring happiness, that give joy, that bring peace and harmony and pleasure to the mind. In innocent enjoyment and happiness is found a spiritual food, which feeds the mind and the soul and makes them more sublime. Only those pleasures are to be avoided which are liable to be productive of pain, sorrow, and regrets. Man must seek to learn what these pleasures are. These and these only is he to deny himself.

Life is a joy. Neither a disease, an evil, nor a curse is it. Life on earth is the beginning of the life that continues. Just as we live the earth life, so shall we continue life after we pass beyond the Veil.

In Nature there is never to be found a sudden interruption of one stage of growth and a jumping into another stage. All things pass through a growth from one stage to another, and in such degree that the change is not even perceptible until it has actually been made.

So is the change between this life and the future life, between this stage of existence and the other. And the soul that lived in the body of him whose mind was filled with thoughts of self-abhorrence, of self-pity, of self-torture, and of disease and the tiredness and the monotony of life, cannot expect to pass from this plane into the realms of light, of joy, of happiness, and of perfection. Growth in light, joy, happiness, and perfection must have its beginning in the earth sphere in order to reach its culmination in the sphere of Perfect Realization. We might as well think of admitting to college courses of study the youth who has completely neglected his elementary training. What would we think of the directors of a college who would enroll a student in Calculus who had no knowledge whatever of the lower grades of mathematics?

And yet there are multitudes of souls who think to be admitted to the world of light and joy who have not an inkling of light and joy in their natures, which could qualify them to endure the light and joy of another world. After degrading the Image of the Father here on earth, after denying it its just needs and dwarfing it through unnatural thoughts and through an abnormal life, think you that they are prepared to enter a land of Perfection and Realization? Think you that the soul thus pinched and dwarfed and starved is prepared to enjoy a world of light, life, and love, where perfection only is supposed to abound?

The New Commandment teaches no such doctrines. It denies the doctrine of self-abasement, and exalts the doctrine of Manhood as the only way to Godhood.

CHAPTER FOUR

Conscious Individuality, the Goal of Life.

The true aim of life is to become a Conscious Individuality, an individual that has realized all the potencies belonging to man. This means development of all departments of the being. Not only must the physical body be perfected and set free from disease and weakness, but the mind also must be developed and set free from erroneous conceptions and false ideas, from harmful desires and destructive appetites, from belief in dogmas and creeds that fetter and bind and make slaves of men.

The attainment of Conscious Individuality demands that man shall become a free man in the true sense of the word, bound to nothing except the truth. Wisdom must be his guide in life, and he must accept only those things which wisdom points out as true and right. Besides freedom of body from disease and weakness and suffering, besides freedom of mind from bondage to the self and to others, there is yet another freedom that man must attain —that is, freedom of soul from bondage to the flesh.

This does not mean that the soul must become a separate entity. Freedom of soul means that the soul must assert itself, must free itself, from the tomb of the flesh, and must enlist the *co-operation of the flesh* in arousing its divine powers. Freedom of soul does not require shaking off the flesh and breaking all connection with it. Rather does it require that there shall be no conflict between the soul and the flesh. They must work in harmony toward one end and one purpose. This is the Great Work placed before man—that soul, mind, and body shall work together and in harmony, to perfect Manhood after the pattern of Godhood. When harmony has been established thus, the soul becomes the Voice of Conscience, which guides man in the right and in the way to wisdom.

Before this state of freedom is reached, it is but natural that man should suffer in many ways. It is scarcely possible for him to attain freedom other than through his own experience; and experience means pain and suffering. Much can be learned through the experience of others; but the Great Work, after all, has to do with the self. And, only through experience, can he learn what is good for him and what is not good. When he learns to discriminate between that which is beneficent and that which is detrimental in its effects, he must then exercise a wise choice. He must select the good and the beneficial, and must reject and deny himself those things which have been the means of bringing suffering and weakness, and of placing him in bondage to them. More than this, he must make conscious effort to strengthen his powers and to become master of negative conditions instead of slaves to them.

These things must he do with a definite goal in mind. This goal may be the attainment of peace and happiness; or it may be the attainment of perfect and complete Manhood, resulting in consciousness of Godhood. These three are virtually identical, each being dependent on the others.

Man may have the notion that peace and happiness come through loss of individuality of self and through entering Nirvana as an unindividualized particle of the Universal Substance. This, however, is a mistaken notion. Individual consciousness, individual attainment, individual growth, individual perfection, individual Manhood, leading to the consciousness of Godhood—this alone gives true peace and happiness. True, by reaching Nirvana, a man may attain a certain freedom from vexation. But it is equally true that this state of freedom from vexation has been attained at the expense of everything that makes man a Man. The peace, or the freedom from vexation, which Nirvana typifies, is gained through self-disintegration and self-deterioration. Whereas, the peace and the happiness advocated by the New Commandment, is gained through self-assertion and self-development, through self-mastery and self-unfoldment, through self-expansion and self-perfection. The Nirvana type of happiness is through *loss* of individuality. The type of happiness advocated by the New Commandment is through *perfection* of individuality.

It is the soul in man, the Divine Spark of divinity within his nature, which makes possible, enjoyment and suffering. Consequently, in order to reach the negative type of peace represented by Nirvana, it is necessary to destroy the Divine Spark so that neither pain nor joy is possible. In establishing the impossibility of pain and joy, man makes of himself an inert machine, incapable of feeling. He destroys all possibility of reaching Godhood and Conscious Individuality, simply because he refuses to accept the possibilities of Manhood, simply because he refuses to accept the possibility of suffering and sorrow and pain. In refusing the possibility of pain, he refuses the possibility of joy; for it is a truth beyond contradiction that the ability to enjoy necessitates the ability to suffer. He who cringes under pain and endeavors to deaden the sensibility that makes pain possible, is, by that very attitude of mind, deadening the sensibility that makes pleasure possible.

There is no law in heaven or on earth to compel one to accept the responsibilities of Manhood. Neither is there a law in heaven or on earth that can make it possible for one to attain Manhood or Godhood without accepting the responsibilities belonging thereto. Shouldering the responsibilities of Manhood entitles one to the rewards of Manhood, entitles one to the strength of Manhood. To endure pain and hardship and suffering and to gain strength through them, is a part of the responsibility of life.

The true human being, he with manhood even partially developed, is willing to accept the responsibility placed upon him as one created in the Divine Image. He is willing to suffer all those things which are given man to suffer, in order that he may gain knowledge thereby. Through the knowledge gained, he shall gradually free himself from weakness. Thus, he gradually develops strength of individuality; and, through overcoming, he gains power to throw off undesirable conditions.

The command, "Be a man and thou mayst become a god," emphasizes the necessity of accepting the responsibilities of life. Through accepting and overcoming, one becomes master of circumstances.

Two paths in life are open to man. With him, rests the choice. Either the one or the other is his.

The one path leads to Manhood, to strength, to Conscious Individuality, eventually, to Godhood, and the power to enjoy all good things without the necessity of accepting suffering.

The other path leads to negativeness, deterioration, inertness, and, ultimately, to loss of individuality and loss of the Divine Spark, which might enable man to attain Godhood. This path leads to a state of mind that can neither suffer nor enjoy. Ultimately, death of the physical body ends all, because the divine image within—that which enables one to receive impressions of joy and of pain— has already been destroyed through refusal to bring it to conscious manifestation.

To seek wisdom and knowledge is one reason why

man is placed here on earth. It is admitted that knowledge brings responsibility with it.   But he who has a
spark of manhood in his nature is willing to accept the responsibility, knowing that responsibility, cheerfully accepted, brings strength, and that strength is power, and that
power means the possibility of possessing peace, contentment, and happiness.

To be sure, there are multitudes who believe in the
doctrine of negativeness, and the doctrine that it is sinful or at least detrimental to seek human knowledge.   But
careful observation reveals that these are under the influence of other minds, and they have hypnotized themselves
into a negative type of peace and happiness.   They are
under the delusion that the bondage they suffer in this life
will prepare for them a place of glory in the Hereafter.

In the same way, we find multitudes who, suffering
from some painful disease, accept the suffering with a
smile, making no effort to be relieved of it, believing that,
by meekly and unquestioningly accepting what comes to
them, they are meeting the conditions of becoming a shin-
ing light in glory and of being robed in a garment of
splendor in the Beyond.

That the doctrine of negativeness is prevalent is a
pity; for it leads to inertness, irresponsiveness, and destructiveness both to body and soul.   By making no effort
to free body and mind from the bondage of sickness and
pain, they fail to develop the soul into a state of Conscious Individuality.   The inert and meek acceptance of
suffering and disease is in violation of the laws of nature,
and of the laws of God, which bid humankind to seek wisdom, first of all, and so to live as to glorify the image of
Him who has created them and has endowed them with the
opportunity to know good from evil, joy from sorrow,
pleasure from pain, freedom from slavery, and, eventually,
to reach the Divine Consciousness.   To seek wisdom and

to endeavor to live in harmony with the laws of nature and the laws of God, prepare one for the time of parting between the earthly house and its tenant. Unless man accepts this responsibility and makes every effort for wisdom, there is but one end. That is, loss of individuality in the state called Nirvana; and that which was, is no more, except in an unconscious, unindividualized, impersonal state.

Human knowledge which really ends in divine knowledge is therefore a truly desirable thing. For, without knowledge, wisdom is impossible; and, without wisdom, man cannot reach individualized consciousness; and, without individualized consciousness, Godhood is impossible, and man finds that he has nothing, is nothing, and ends in nothing.

As already indicated, the New Commandment advocates that man shall become an individuality, conscious of its oneness with the All Father. This is the ultimate goal placed before him. The New Commandment advocates gaining knowledge of both heaven and earth. More than this, it advocates that it is wise for man to make use of his natural instincts.

The negative philosophy, that which, if followed, ends in nothingness, teaches that to have regard for natural instinct is to court death, and to forfeit peace and happiness in the world to come.

The New Commandment, on the contrary, advocates following the natural instincts in a natural, normal manner, not allowing them to become perverted nor to become the master.

One of the natural instincts is hunger. To satisfy natural hunger in a normal manner, is desirable as well as necessary. To refuse to satisfy hunger because of the notion that the soul is ennobled by suffering hunger, is to pervert a natural instinct. On the other hand, to give

unnecessary and unnatural food to the system, is, likewise, a perversion of natural instinct. By neither method
do we ennoble the Divine Image. By either method we
mar the Image of Divinity; and to continue in such an
unnatural course is to destroy the whole structure.

Another natural instinct is the desire for strength
and power. And to seek strength and power through natural means, such as proper food, proper work and exercise, proper self-culture, and other measures, is to glorify
the Divine Image inherent in man. This soon becomes
apparent through beauty of character and through the joy-
radiating influences of one's being.

It is a natural instinct to crave pleasure and joy.
When this craving can be gratified without harm to the self
or others, results are divine, and ennobling to the entire
being. But, to refuse a reasonable gratification of the
desire for pleasure and joy under the mistaken idea that
self-denial in this respect is noble, is a perversion of natural instinct, and leads to harm and self-injury. This is
negativeness. It is slavery to a dogma that has no foundation, and the end thereof is deterioration of the Divine
Image in man's nature.

A doctrine kindred to the doctrine of self-denial is
that of self-affliction, or self-torture. Natural instincts,
unsatisfied and denied, become perversions of the worst
type. The negative doctrine of denial leads to self-affliction. This is natural; for, if one believes in the doctrine
of self-denial in regard to natural instincts, naturally he
either perverts his instincts or tries to deaden them. If
he succeeds in deadening them, these forces, which were
positive forces when they demanded gratification, have now
through self-denial, become negative forces. Man who
was formerly a positive being has now become a negative
being. Such a man will naturally believe that all those
things which have to do with the earth life are evil and

should be denied. Consequently, he will be afraid to do anything, lest it may be wrong, since strength and manhood, wisdom and knowledge, pleasure and joy, are to be avoided. Man cannot live without doing something. It follows that self-affliction to such a diseased mind becomes the natural thing. To such a mind, this is an honor to God. In this way, a crown of glory and a robe of light are to be received immediately on becoming free from the flesh.

All nature teaches contrary to this doctrine. Through natural gratification of natural instincts in a natural manner, joy and happiness are gained. Through normal use of normal powers, additional strength is gained. All nature teaches this. When natural appetites are gratified in a natural manner, strength and beauty result therefrom. Also, the possibility of obtaining still greater strength and beauty results. This may continue indefinitely until perfection is reached.

It is not necessary for man to possess a large amount of wealth in order to realize the highest state of strength or happiness. Granted, a certain amount of possessions is necessary in order that he may have the things needful for right living. But it is also true that, if a man is willing to free himself from weakness and is willing to use his strength and wisdom for good, he will be able to obtain the things he desires, and with every new effort come possessions, until there is an accumulation of the necessities of life, just as there is an accumulation of power, of strength, of knowledge, and of individuality.

But the first requisite is freedom. In serfdom there is no power. In serfdom is no possibility of obtaining power and individuality, or happiness and the necessities of life. So long as man is content to be the slave either of himself or of others, just that long will be denied to him those things, whether it be time, opportunity, or money, which he requires in order to become what he should be.

When man seeks knowledge, first of all, when he makes use of his knowledge for good, when he seeks to learn his weaknesses in order to replace them with strength, when he seeks to find the cause of his servitude in order to remove it—then will he free himself and become master instead of slave, a man instead of a weakling; and, gradually, he will become one with God rather than one with negativeness and destructiveness and perversity of nature.

Wealth alone can give man neither freedom, health, happiness, nor pleasure. He may possess wealth incalculable and still be diseased and in misery. If he obeys the laws that will free him from disease and will build up health, if he lives so as to be free from an accusing conscience, he may be happy in spite of a meagre supply of material possessions. Freedom from all undesirable things is the goal for man to reach.

Such freedom comes through Conscious Individuality, and through the development of conscious Unity with Deity, in His varied and manifold aspects. "Let us lay aside every weight and the sin that doth so easily beset us and run with patience the race that is set before us"— even the race that leads to true Manhood, eventually, to true Godhood and the Deific Consciousness.

CHAPTER FIVE

It Is Not Necessary to Renounce the World and Its Possessions.

To a certain extent at least, earthly possessions are absolutely necessary in this age for the peace and the well-being of man. Without a reasonable degree of them it is not possible for man to be at his best, nor is it possible for him to bring the potential power within himself into manifestation.

A reasonable independence in regard to the necessities of life should be sought by him who wishes to attain the highest development of his powers. Human relationships are not to be shunned. The duties and the cares of a home are to be welcomed. To avoid or to shun or to shrink from them is to forfeit the right to the joys and the pleasures of a home. To have amiable friends and agreeable acquaintances demands a price. But these very things are above all else the most truly "worth while," and are deserving of the highest price. To meet the requirements of business relationships with others, of social relationships, aye, even of home and domestic relationships, demands a positive attitude.

The positive life is the only kind of life that is of any consequence; and, every day, it becomes more apparent that the positive attitude is absolutely necessary to enable one to meet the requirements of the varied functions and conditions of life.

Let no one gather erroneous impressions regarding the term, "positive attitude." Positive attitude in no wise means supercilious officiousness in one's relations with others. Nor does it in any degree suggest the haughty spirit of "better than thou." Neither is it marked by obstinate determination to have one's own way.

Let it be emphasized from many points of view that the positive attitude first and foremost means mastery within oneself. It means self-control. It means firmness with reference to one's own thoughts, feelings, words, and acts. The positive attitude exercises authority over one's powers and forces, directing them into proper, carefully approved channels, conserving, rather than dissipating and diffusing, them. The positive being is one who cheerfully and faithfully accepts the responsibilities of life, one who encourages only wholesome, constructive thoughts and happy, optimistic views. The positive character is willing to take his place in social and community interests and to bear his share of their burdens. The positive being is courageous and shrinks not from facing difficulties and hardships. He meets conditions bravely, knowing that all responsibilities, faithfully met, add to one's fund of useful experience. With the one of positive attitude, so-called failures and reverses act only as spurs to goad him on to more persistent effort and to a more determined search for wisdom in regard to the practical things of life.

The positive attitude is the opposite of negativeness, inertness, and indifference. It is the opposite of slave-like complacency and inactivity. The positive attitude is self-assertive in its effort to become qualified and equipped for the duties of life and for the requirements of a chosen profession or career.

God, the Great Creator of all, manifests Himself to man through a positive nature. He is by no means a negative being, but is continually creative. This fact becomes a constant reminder to man that he likewise is creative only in proportion as he is of a positive nature. To succeed in life demands creative ability, and it is therefore necessary to be positive. One must make his plans and hold firmly to them. One must not allow himself to become the dupe of circumstances and conditions. Even though one may not be able to change circumstances and conditions, he can at least master himself in the midst of them and extract good from them. This demands a positive attitude. This demands the use of creative faculties and self-assertiveness.

The positive attitude does not renounce the world and worldly possessions. Rather than regarding it a mark of spirituality to renounce them, the positive attitude considers it a mark of negativeness. To meet the requirements of business interests and to solve the problems incident thereto, demands positiveness and self-assertiveness—the very qualities that make for spirituality and power. Therefore, if one shuns the responsibilities attendant upon earthly interests, he is, by that very attitude of mind, neglecting attributes and powers which are essential to the higher growth. One should welcome these responsibilities as a necessary means of growth.

Time has been when it was possible for man to live a normal life, even though he had no fixed habitation. But that time is passed; and, with few exceptions, man must see to it that he has a settled abiding place, called home. This requires the necessities of life and earthly possessions and human relationships. Humble and modest, indeed, these may be. But the tomorrow will not take care of itself unless man exercises creative ability in providing for the tomorrow. He must know whence comes the next meal, whence comes protection against frost, wind, and snow. Even though human relationships be the most normal and natural possible, even though provisions be simple and inexpensive, yet forethought and skill are required to meet the needs of every-day life.

Far from true is it that, in order to strive for the

Higher Life, the Soul Life, it is necessary to renounce earthly possessions. Rather than being wrong to enjoy that which has been honestly earned, it is a benefit to the aspirant after wisdom and soul power to have a reasonable degree of earthly possessions to enjoy. To have a home which one has been able to equip with the necessities and the comforts of life, to have the assurance that one need not worry for the day to come, relieves one's mind and enables one to give undivided attention and thought to the greater work in hand. Thus, earthly comforts become a real benefit to the Higher Life.

There is, however, no ground for discouragement to him who has life before him, who is just beginning his work, but is destitute of the necessities and the comforts of life. For, if he has true manhood, if he is not a slave to conditions or to others or to himself, he will soon gain these benefits.

In the present age of efficiency, every man who is willing to be truly Man, can think and plan, execute and produce, with honest labor, more than is required for each day's comforts. Consequently, it is possible for him to lay by something each day, so that in good time there may be an accumulation from which to give himself and those dependent on him, some of the pleasures and enjoyments of life. If he does not accomplish this, it is evident that he is not planning and working wisely or that he is the slave of circumstances and conditions or of some one who has learned to take from him that which is his. In that case, it is his first duty to seek wisdom and knowledge, to learn the cause of his failure, and then to rectify the error.

Moreover, it is neither honorable nor wise, nor is it the will of the All Father, that one man should give to another that which rightly belongs to himself. It is right to give to those who are unfortunate in ways they cannot avoid; but to give to those who are as able to help themselves as we are, is only to harm them. Charity is a noble quality of heart; but indiscriminate giving may be productive of harm to those whom we seek to help.

With few exceptions, all men are born with potential strength, wisdom, and ability. Some, nevertheless, give way to a weak, negative, morbid nature, and refuse to work for the necessities of life. They yield to negativeness under the mistaken notion that the life of complacency and inactivity, the life that works not, enjoys not, and gains not, is the life that receives a sublime recompense in the world to come. It is neither right nor just for such as these to be sustained by those who believe in the creative, constructive life, who have earned their possessions by making use of the powers God has given to all men. He who wishes to give of his means or his possessions to a noble and worthy cause, because he is able to give and has the inclination to give, will be rewarded by the Divine Law, "It is more blessed to give than to receive." But "the blessedness" of giving does not apply to indiscriminate support of those who are qualified to help themselves, but do not, because of belief in negative doctrines.

Man is made in the image of the Father, and is supposed to be at his best when he imitates the Father. It is but natural that he should pattern after his heavenly Father. He soon learns that the Father gives nothing to His children unless they work for it, even though they may believe in an inactive life. Unless the farmer plows the field, and sows the wheat, cuts the grain and mills it, he has no bread. It matters not how many acres of the best land the farmer may possess, it matters not how incessantly he may pray for daily bread, it remains a fact that bread comes not unless the land is tilled or honest effort in some other way is made to secure daily bread.

Bread is earned through creative work of some kind. We only plunge another into greater weakness by giving him that which he should gain through his own efforts.

Does the mother bird teach her young to fly by continually carrying them on her back?

It is the negative being, laboring under a misconception of life and its possibilities, that thinks it righteous and godly to renounce earthly possessions.

To be sure, as in all other matters, there is an extreme to be guarded against. To bend all one's energies to the obtaining of earthly treasures, defiles the image in which man is created. This extreme is as serious as the opposite extreme of renouncing them. Neither extreme is satisfactory. "The golden mean," the desire for possessions sufficient for a righteous and full life, is both just and honorable, and keeps man from becoming a parasite and a vampire on society.

The vital admonition of the Law is, "Seek ye first the kingdom of heaven." That is, seek to bring into activity all the powers within your being. Develop the mind and the thinking faculties. Mellow the heart so that love and wisdom shall be therein. Help the Divine Spark to spring forth and to blossom as the rose. Use your creative powers, your manhood, to obtain those things which are necessary to peace of mind, strength of body, and happiness of heart. This is reason. This is justice. This is wisdom. This is doing what man is intended to do.

Goodness of heart, greatness of soul, loftiness of mind, and generosity of spirit can never come through denying the self earthly possessions. Nor can they come through the wearing of tatters, nor through refusing to think of earthly interests, nor through being a negative, feelingless creature, tossed about by every wind of doctrine. Goodness of heart, greatness of soul, loftiness of mind, generosity of spirit—these qualities come through doing the duties that belong to manhood, through using every power of mind in the creative work for which it was intended, through accepting the responsibilities of life, through working and doing, even doing things that are not to our liking, but doing them faithfully because they fall to our lot to do. These are the things that give man power and force. These are the things that bring satisfaction.

He who is afraid to undertake the duties of life for fear of failure already confesses himself a failure. He confesses himself to be in bondage to fear. Bondage to his own fear will eventually put him in bondage to others to be exploited by them.

The same Law that bids, "Seek ye the kingdom of heaven," also encourages us to seek an earthly home and a reasonable degree of earthly pleasures and earthly possessions. Few indeed there are who find the kingdom of heaven who do not also find a home and earthly enjoyments; for the same power, the same capabilities, the same mental attitude, which helps man find the kingdom of heaven, also helps him to make a home for himself. The New Commandment encourages the cultivation of affection and love and devotion and faithfulness—even affection and love for things of the earth, and devotion and faithfulness to earthly relationships. But it strikes the note of warning against an excess of attachment to earthly conditions, a warning against holding earthly possessions as idols. Thou shalt have no other god before the All Father.

The love of man for his family and for his home and for the conditions that make an ideal home, is to be commended. If a man loves these things, then we may take it for granted that he will do his duty toward them; and, in this way, he honors his God and Creator. But, if a man makes an idol of any possessions, he thereby

breaks the divine command, by thinking only of his possessions and forgetting the Father of all. Through becoming absorbed in the earthly treasure, he loses sight of
the counter-part of God, which is within his own being,
he forgets the Divine Spark of divinity within his own
nature, and fails to bring it into manifestation.

But so long as the Divine Nature holds the first and
greatest love in his heart, it is wise and right for him to
bestow affection and attention upon earthly possessions;
for, by taking care of these things, he cultivates and encourages the higher love. Through the care of earthly
interests and protection for them, he develops manhood
and learns wisdom.

Three classes of men people the earth.

The one class is of the negative type. They have
the abnormal belief that it is wrong to use their creative,
constructive powers. They refuse to develop their potential energies and latent forces. They live upon the
efforts of others, or, it may be, they serve and obey others.
Their lives are negative, inert, ambitionless, unproduc-
tive. Those, however, upon whom they live gain their
livelihood through the use of constructive, positive faculties.

Another class have learned to know the powers they
possess and to use them in creative and productive channels. More than this, they have learned to lay hold of
the negative class of society and use them to their own
selfish interests. They enslave them under hard labor
and strenuous toil, giving them, in compensation, barely
enough to keep soul and body together.

The third class is of those who accept the Divine
Law as their standard. In the beginning, this class suffer
severely; for it is through experience that they learn.
But, by accepting every experience as a lesson that is
well to master, they apply its message to their need and

go in search for wisdom and knowledge. They condemn neither conditions nor personalities, but gradually free themselves from every form of bondage.

They free themselves from weakness of body and endeavor to live in such a manner that freedom from disease is obtained.

Freedom of mind also they strive after. They seek to learn the truth. And, having found a satisfactory interpretation, they cling to it, regardless of whether others understand it as they do. Nor do they care if the truth as they understand it is condemned by others or is not in harmony with established beliefs. To them it is truth. And they are free enough to know that it is to their advantage to be faithful to their best understanding of truth regardless of what others think. Nevertheless, firmness in regard to their own convictions is tempered with mildness and kindness, and freedom from condemnation of others; and there is no inclination in their hearts to judge others harshly as to their beliefs, words, ways, or acts. Firmness in regard to themselves, mildness and kindness in regard to others—these are essentials of the positive attitude of mind.

This class also is eager in its search after freedom of soul. They desire to learn what is constructive and good, and what is destructive and harmful. They develop a power of will that enables them to select and to choose the good and the constructive. Thus, gradually, they evolve true manhood; and with it comes freedom— a freedom so powerful that no one is strong enough to take it from them or to interfere with it.

Individual men, evolving thus from the state of weakness and servitude into freedom and mastery, in time, constitute a class of society. In proportion as this class grows, the other two classes must give way. Thus in a slow, gradual, but sure manner, the regeneration of mankind takes place. This is the aim and the goal placed before humanity. It rests with each individual to accept the ideal of freedom and true manhood for himself. As he succeeds in his aim, others are inspired to follow his example, until, through the sweep of centuries, mankind generally has adopted the ideal of manhood and true freedom, which lead ultimately to individualized Godhood.

To the one who has reached this type of freedom and manhood, of mastership, nothing is prohibited; for it is his privilege as the reward of self-mastership to be a co-worker with God, and to possess all good things on the earth. To be sure, with no one does freedom mean license to do as he pleases, whether good or not good. The highest freedom has not been reached until man's choice is guided by a wisdom that keeps him "in the narrow way" of right and justice and goodness.

Who can say there are no good things on the earth for man to enjoy? At the present day, in the present age, the opportunities for peace and happiness, the opportunities for the possession of those things which bring joy and contentment, are greater than they have ever been in the history of the world. But, in order to possess them, we must show that we are worthy of them. For they are given only to those who earn them whether by their own efforts or by the ability to direct others in earning them.

It is wisdom for us to strive after manhood in the fullest and truest sense of the word, and to bring forth all our potential powers into manifestation, and thus become worthy of possessions, worthy of living in the Age of Divine Realization, worthy of being in the Divine Image, worthy of Sonship with the Father.

CHAPTER SIX

Hope, the elevating magnet of life.

The hope of attaining that which we desire and which we believe we can attain and claim, is the thing that stimulates man to action. Without the desire to attain, there will be nothing to hope for. Without desire, without hope, man is a mere nothing, bound straight for Nirvana—that is, reabsorption in the great storehouse of that which IS, but is not individual, so that those who again become part of the storehouse straightway lose their individuality.

Without desires, there is no hope, except possibly the hope of death. And the desires of man are legion in their variety. Most of the desires of man are natural desires. That is to say, they are normal desires, and, if gratified, can lead only to good.

The desire for death is an unnatural desire. It causes man to become wholly negative. This negative state, like the opium-habit, leads him to think that he has no desires, when, in fact, this very delusion leads to many desires, which are, nevertheless, perversions of natural, normal desires. Living under a false belief, a false conception of life and human destiny, and viewing things in the wrong light, regarding that which is natural to man as something to be avoided, the negative, hopeless man soon comes to see the abnormal and the perverse as something desirable. And, under the pessimistic eye of a nature perverted by negative doctrines, virtue becomes a thing to be shunned, and perversity becomes desirable.

Between vice and virtue, between strength and weakness, there is only the difference of direction. The fountain is the same for both. The center is the same, but the channel through which the forces flow is different. One is natural, normal, desirable; the other is totally unnatural and perverse.

In the time of youth and construction, desire and the hope of accomplishment is the incentive to life. Desire and its attendant hope is a noble quality of soul—aye, it is even divine. For, through desire, all the impulses of life are awakened and set into motion; and, through continual motion, all that is good is accomplished.

In old age, it is natural to forget the desires of youth or to find that earlier desires are dead and that only one desire remains—the desire for peace and inaction. But in the youth or in the mature man, the desire for inaction is abnormal, and leads to vice and to those things which are detrimental and destructive, not only to the self, but to others as well.

In youth, there are many desires, and there is the eternal hope of accomplishment. The stronger the desires in the heart of man, the greater is the hope of their realization. To the normal man, the hope of realizing his desires, always for the best interest of himself, and those near and dear to him, is like a star in the heavens, ever drawing him onward and upward, until, at last, through effort, he has been able to reach the star that has been guiding him and beckoning him on. Furthermore, no sooner will he have reached the first star than there will be another star to attract him. Aye, possibly, long before the first great desire has been realized, another desire has been forming, a desire for greater accomplishment than the light of the first star pointed out. And, just as soon as the first desire has been realized, it is straightway forgotten, and another desire, the gleam of another star, leads him on to still greater achievement.

This is natural desire and its star of hope. That it is both normal and divine is seen in the fact that, without desire and without hope, nothing is accomplished. Again, the normal and divine nature of desire and hope is seen in the fact that, in the realization and the accomplishment of a great desire, there is neither time nor inclination nor opportunity for weakness and vice, since all one's time and strength and thought are occupied in the accomplishment of the work in view.

This is the doctrine of manhood. No great school or educational system is needed to teach the lad, the youth, the man in his prime, that he should entertain some great desire. For, if he is natural and normal, or, if he is healthy, there will be healthy desires in his breast; and, unless these desires are perverted through false teachings, there is little danger of his going astray.

Manhood and the works of manhood constitute the theme of the new age, the age that is just beginning. Fear is giving way to the desire to accomplish and the desire to become. No longer will the healthy man be held in bondage by erroneous teachings, religious and philosophical teachings, which have held the human race back for long centuries past, making man afraid to think for himself, still more afraid to act for himself. The fear that has characterized the past age is due to the false teaching that, if man should make a grievous mistake, it is possible he may be damned for eternity. The age of fear passes away with the age of false ideas concerning desire and the accomplishment of desire.

No longer will man be bound to the doctrine, East-founded, that the supreme virtue is to kill out all desire and to substitute in the place of the many desires that may actuate a being, the one desire to be rid of all things, to be rid of human responsibilities—in short, to be a leaf on the human tree, to be blown here and there, to be

used as a slave, to have every sense perverted and changed into weak, Nirvana-bound inertness, which lives and
dies, and shall be no more.

The new age teaches manhood, in the true sense of
the word. It teaches man to think, to desire, to plan; and,
above all, it teaches him to execute his plans, to *do,* even
if, in the doing, he must go through hells of fire in order
to accomplish. For it is by doing, by suffering, if necessary, because of the determination to accomplish, that
man becomes more of man, and through manhood eventually reaches the consciousness of Godhood.

The doctrine of the new age has no compliment for
the coward, the negative being, who fears to do anything
lest he may do wrong. It is signally true that those who
fear to do are the very ones who are continually doing
wrong, doing that which tends toward self-destructiveness;
since to do nothing because of fear is a greater evil
than to make a mistake while trying to do right. He who
continually fears that, through desiring some particular
object or through desiring to accomplish some particular
thing, he may be doing that which is wrong or detrimental to himself, is, through that very attitude of mind, reap-
ing harm more than he would by striving earnestly to
realize the desire. To such an one, life is like the serpent in the grass, ever ready to lead him astray, ever
ready to lead him to that which he fears is the hell of
eternity. Such an one forgets that only he reaches the
state of nothingness who hesitates and fears to undertake
the responsibilities of manhood. On the other hand, to
him who accepts bravely the responsibilities of manhood,
life is the serpent of wisdom, which directs him into
pleasant paths.

Moreover, negative thoughts gradually change the
polarity of the brain until at last the negative being can
think no other thoughts than those of the pessimistic

type. Eventually, he arrives at the stage in which he sees the morbid and the destructive as right, while perversity of thought, desire, and act become to him as virtues to be followed. This is the delusion of a mind that has fallen into the negative state.

Hope is not vanity and a snare. Hope is glorious and sublime. Hope is not merely the anticipation of a happy state in the future, but also the expectancy of success in the present life. For the future in both this and the next plane is founded upon the success of the present. He who does not endeavor to live a natural, normal, healthful life here and now, he who does not achieve in the present sphere, will not be given the opportunity to achieve in another world. For the earth plane is the testing school of God wherein souls are tried and either found strong and willing *to do and to dare* or else found wanting and cast back into the ocean of universal substance, there to lose individuality and consciousness.

He cannot hope to meet with success, in whose breast is found the fear to do, where desire and hope should be. It is the desire and the hope to be or to do that stimulates man to act. If the desire is strong enough, not even a doubt in regard to accomplishment presents itself to his mind.

In every heart, unless totally depraved, there is a spark, which, when aroused to life and activity, is a mighty power for good. There are, in fact, two diverse desires— the one is a desire for accomplishment, the other is a fear that it may not be right to accomplish. The latter has not always been a part of man; but, gradually, through the ages, by reason of the negative doctrines, it has found lodgment in his nature. But let it be a cause of encouragement that the spark of good and noble desire is native to the soil of the human heart, and that it may be nurtured into a mighty Flame of pure unselfishness, which shines as a light in darkness.

The negativeness found today in many, often called pessimism, is nothing more nor less than the germ of old age and decay in the heart of youth. It is only natural that the aged man should not be concerned about accomplishment and should look forward to peace and rest. He has passed through the age of desire and hope, into, and through, the age of work and accomplishment; consequently, he is not at the stage of life in which fulfillment is looked for. But to find the germ of negativeness in the young man as it naturally appears in the aged man, is to be deplored.

Negativeness is the natural and inevitable result of erroneous teachings, false philosophy, and religion—teachings which make of the human heart a coward, rather than the strong character one should be. The responsibility for negativeness in man's nature is to be laid at the door of those philosophies which teach him that it is necessary to kill out all earthly desires, in order to attain the state of bliss in a world to come. This abnormal teaching, this perverted idea, has gradually sown the seed of negativeness and cowardice, and has made of man almost universally a weak, negative, slave-like creature.

The negative doctrine is the doctrine of the darkness of death, the doctrine of the night of life, when an age, once young and strong and pure, gradually came to the end of time, and when the youth of time had gradually passed away, and with its passing left the thoughts and desires of old age.

But the age of negativeness is passing away, and the age of manhood and positiveness is being ushered in. Not all of that which is dead has been buried and forgotten, yet much of it has been relegated to the past as cast-off and outgrown garments. The youth of the new age is growing up, becoming strong, making use of the new doctrine, obeying the New Command, and positiveness and manhood are becoming the rule rather than the exception.

Under the power of positive thought and positive life, society will soon be marked by two classes of individuals. One class will continue to follow the old belief that it is wrong to assert manhood and to strengthen normal desires, and will become a slave to that which is negative, perverted, dark, and lifeless, thus becoming slaves to stronger wills. The other class, having learned that only manhood and self-assertion pays, will give heed to the New Commandment, will strengthen desire and concentration, will follow the star of hope and go forward in the work.

In the pessimist, the natural elements are perverted. The perversions may be due to several causes. In some, perversity of nature may be attributed to hereditary conditions. In others, it may be ascribed to erroneous teachings. In still others, environment may be responsible for abnormal tendencies. While, in many, a combination of causes may account for perverse and negative conditions.

Even so, there is within each individual a voice or an instinct that pictures the active life as the only truly desirable life to live. A mighty effort is required to free the self from the bonds of slavery, especially the slavery of thought. Nevertheless, if man is willing to pay the price, he can free himself from all objectionable fetters. It is the work and the message and the duty of the New Commandment to show even the most negative and degraded man how to assert the power inherent within himself, so as to gain freedom from every type of undesirable bondage.

The one great, throbbing, seemingly vital factor to be overcome in the mind and the heart of man is fear. It is fear in some form or another that holds the multitudes in bondage, preventing them from making an effort, stopping them on the very threshold of manhood.

Fear comes in various guises. A very common guise is the belief that certain desires are wrong: that desire for normal conquest, even conquest that is not at the expense of others, is wrong; that desire for earthly love causes one to be denied heavenly love; that earthly possessions forfeit heavenly treasures; that effort in a worldly way precludes heavenly reward. Such ideas as these, abnormal and tantalizing fears, are the means of preventing man from making the start in the Higher Life, preventing him from throwing off the shackles of serfdom and putting on the mantle of manhood.

There is but one way to overcome—that is, *to be a Man.* Make up your mind that you care nothing whether it will mean destruction of soul and body or salvation of both, but that, come what will, you will make the start, that you will do things, that you will desire, hope, and accomplish, come what will. When the mind once becomes charged with a determination such as this, when man begins to work in keeping with his determination, then, things will be accomplished. When all that is negative and destructive in nature finds that it cannot enslave the mind, then, that which was formerly a negative, inert nature becomes a source of power; for Nature must first be completely overcome, before she will become the mistress of man and do his bidding.

CHAPTER SEVEN

Suppress a natural desire, and it becomes a vice.

The normal youth, as well as the normal person of middle age, is full of the desires that naturally form a part of the life of man. These desires are manifold, and embrace almost every department of nature. Some of these have to do with the natural instincts, while others concern the possessions that are necessary in order to make life worth living. Each man is a law unto himself, and the desires of each individual differ to a greater or lesser extent.

Now it is not possible for all of the desires of man to be followed; for it is often the case that very different or even conflicting desires throb in the human heart at the same time. In this case, it becomes a matter of choice and selection rather than repression. To suppress a desire merely means that another desire takes its place. Normal desire is to be compared to a spring or stream of water. If the channel of the spring or stream is unimpeded, the water remains clear and pure. But, if the channel is obstructed, the water becomes stagnant and poisonous. Just so with human desires. Suppress them and they become stagnant. A suppressed desire becomes stagnant desire; and a stagnant desire breaks out in a vice. It is for this reason, above all else, that negative doctrines are doing an untold harm. All doctrines, whether religious or philosophical, which teach that earthly desires are destructive, and that one can gain eternal life only through suppression of them, are doing an immense amount of harm. Those who accept this doc-

trine, first of all become inert, desiring nothing; then this
very inertness breaks out in a vice that poisons everything
noble in the human being. From it results the lowest
forms of life—it may be even the beggar that walks the
streets, who cares for nothing, loves nothing, looks forward to nothing, except a place to sleep and sufficient
to satisfy immediate hunger. As to his morality, men
who have studied the question know that nowhere on
earth is to be found deeper or more deplorable vice than
among this class of people.

The New Commandment teaches that the religious
and philosophical beggar is not a whit superior to the beggar of the streets. The one walks the earth, caring for
nothing except to eat and sleep. The other teaches that
the way to eternal happiness is by the way of *no-desire,*
by the way of caring for nothing, seeking not earthly
happiness or joy, because it involves care and responsibility. In fact, the beggar of the street is preferable because he seldom imparts to others his destructive ideas.

The way of strength is the way of responsibility.
The way of responsibility is nature's way of making use
of the manifold desires that spring up in the human breast
—a way that is noble and divine, a way that will lead to
success, to happiness, to manhood. This path to power
is not strewn with human wrecks, nor is it marked by
those who have become lepers of morality through suppression of desire. This path is for the youth and the
man of mature age who has selected one supreme desire from the manifold desires that have had power over
him, and who is willing to bend all his energies toward
the realization of this one chosen ambition.

To select one supreme desire as the predominating
power in one's life, does not mean the suppression of former or lesser desires. On the contrary, the lesser desires
find satisfaction in the accomplishment of the greater. All

lesser desires are used, transmuted, changed, in the task of realizing the greater. This is natural, normal development. It develops true manhood through the royal road of work, of accomplishment, of responsibility; and it makes truly a man and not a weakling. Of a truth, there are many paths that lead to accomplishment, but the path of effort, of responsibility, of service, is the only safe path. The one who is morally weak will find it a hard road to travel. It will not allow him the ease and the inertness of a life of idleness and indecision. But, when one is well along the path, his former weaknesses will have passed away; and he will enter the fight with zeal. Nature will cause him to feel that he is in the right, that he is using creative energy, which must eventually bring success if he continues faithful to the right.

The path of energy and positiveness is a difficult path also for the physically weak. Theirs is not the strength to cope with conditions and to show forth good results. But if one is faithful, every trial, every test, every failure, will give greater strength, until, in good time, he will discover that progress is being made, and that strength and power are his. A new trial after a failure is easier than was the former trial; and, like others, he realizes that success and happiness are for those who overcome, and not for those who take all things as they are, without an effort to remove the cause of failures and reverses. In strength and victory, he is far superior to those who, from fear of failure, make no attempt whatever.

He who tries to suppress the desires natural to man, gradually comes to a stage in which he is weary of all things. The earth is an undesirable place to live. Even the thought of heaven has lost its charm. The suppression of normal desires, the suppression of desires for earthly pleasure and enjoyment, has killed out its counterpart—the desire for bliss, for happiness, in a future state.

Suppression of desire is a deadly poison. It poisons not only the body, but the heart and the soul as well. It quenches the fires of the soul. It destroys the creative energy of the mind. It kills manhood, and there is little left of the human being except the body and a diseased condition. True it is that, where there are desires for things of the earth, and where there is joy, there will also be the companion of joy—that is, sorrow. True it is that he who desires and loves and knows keen enjoyment will feel sorrow keenly. True it is that, for those who know, and who have acute sensibilities, there is more sorrow than joy. All this is freely admitted. But who is so weak as to forfeit success for fear of the possibility of a loss? What normal and healthy person would refuse to love and be loved, simply because of the possibility of losing love?

Indeed, there are some who will shun a joy because a sorrow may follow. But the true man, the strong man, the man that would know Immortality, will accept the blessings of today and will not borrow trouble for tomorrow. He has known joy, and is willing to know joy, realizing full well that sorrow, even if it does come, cannot last forever, and that the joy he has once known may be known again.

Moreover, sorrow, like its twin, joy, is for a purpose. The purpose is not only to strengthen, but to give experience and knowledge. He who shrinks from the attainment of experience and knowledge is not a complete man. The normal man invites conditions which test one's strength. He is not willing to pass anything by, which might be to his advantage. He does not hide himself away in seclusion, in order to avoid a disagreeable experience. On the contrary, he marks a path to be trod, and follows it to the end, no matter what may befall him. For life is an experience, a school; and an attempt to evade, to pass something, is to be forced to return again and again, until the character is well rounded and the destiny of existence is fulfilled.

The man who is normally and naturally born is full of desires; and, for every desire, there is potential power. The desire is proof of a power to accomplish according to the desire. If man does not accomplish, it is because he has abused the talents with which God has endowed him. To the man, normally born, with a fair degree of health, and a natural desire to have and to do, are entrusted certain talents. If he is truly a man, and if his mind is not poisoned with false and destructive doctrines, he will make use of the talents given him by bringing his desires into manifestation by good works. As his desires are satisfied and realized and worked out, desires for greater achievement take their place. These also he executes, and becomes an honor to God and to himself and to his fellow men. He gains in manhood and makes progress toward Godhood.

On the other hand, the man born into the world with normal physical powers and normal desires, who does not bring his desires and potentialities into manifestation either because of indifference or because of belief in a negative philosophy, is like the one in the Biblical parable who buried his talent for fear of losing it, and then charged the master with being "a hard master." Such an one is not a true man, manhood is not part of him. He is a weakling and a coward, and not to be classed as one of the children of the Father. He has made the will of the Father null and void. He has robbed himself of his own lawful inheritance.

True it is that the master is a hard master to those who disobey His divine laws. His laws are so clear and plain that no one can say he did not understand. The first requisite of life is health and strength. To gain this is man's first duty. A reasonable degree of health and strength is within the reach of all. It is only required to follow the clear markings of Nature. Her laws are plain, simple, and easily followed. Their name is "Simplicity in all things."

As man becomes master, as he approaches manhood's true estate, he nears the danger line. It is a fact well known to all who have travelled the path of constructiveness, that a sense of self-sufficiency and of individuality is attended by a danger peculiar to itself. It may incline one to separate himself from human help and from human need. One may feel that he is no longer in need of human association and human assistance. This is a great mistake. No one can stand utterly alone. This is the stage in development that demands careful watchfulness. Even though it might be possible for one to live comparatively to himself and satisfy his own needs, yet the Great Law is that as one has attained the higher consciousness, so much the more should he remain among mankind, openly and freely helping them and pointing out the way to them. Though it may not be necessary for him to be in active association with the multitudes, it is, nevertheless, necessary for him to form a bond of unity and to work with others who are of like thought and like interests. When individualists form a bond and become united, the greatest power for good results.

To accept individuality and power as an indication that we should free ourselves from others, and should separate ourselves from those whose inclinations are foreign to ours, thus hiding the light that should shine, would be to defeat the very end and aim of mastership. In a short time, this very isolation and separateness would result in destroying the individuality. Any power, energy, or potency that is allowed to lie dormant through non-use will become weak because it is not put to its test. As the

animal that hibernates, living on its own fat and its own
strength, by the time spring returns, is weak and lean, so
does the mystic become emaciated and lifeless, who uses
not his powers to the benefit of humanity.

A power, an energy, or a faculty, once gained, must
be constantly put to the test in order to keep up its own
strength. The Divine Law is so absolute that, when this
is done, additional strength is given to it. But, if it is
allowed to lie dormant even for a short time, its strength
and resistent powers are reduced. If it remains dormant
for too long a time, all its potency, energy, and power are
lost, and it becomes again as it was in the beginning. The
life of the ordinary human being illustrates this principle.
Coming into the world without power and without strength,
he grows into strength, power, and beauty; but, through
ignorance of the Law, when reaching the height of power,
he begins to weaken and decline, until in the end he is
no stronger than at the time of birth.

This process of accumulating, using, and declining
of strength and power, men generally have considered as
natural, simply because of the false philosophy, the race
belief, that it is a natural, normal process. At the same
time, nevertheless, we have been taught that man is a
prototype of God, having His power in a potential state,
though in a less degree. We are forgetful of the fact
that He in whose image man is created is today the same
as He was centuries ago, and that He has, in no wise,
declined in power or creative ability. We are forgetful
of the fact that it is inconsistent for man, made in the
likeness of the Divine, to pass through the stage of decline—all because of false, destructive, negative philosophy and teachings, an utterly false race belief in the
necessity of weakness, decline, and death.

CHAPTER EIGHT

Servitude Follows Weakness.

When the individual loses his manhood, at that moment he descends to a state of bondage, selling himself, though possibly unconsciously, into serfdom.

In like manner, the moment a nation loses its sense of manhood and strength, at that moment does it begin to decay and to decline; and, at once, other nations begin to rule it, to hold sway over it, and gradually to subjugate it. That this is so, take, for example, India, with its vast millions of people, many times more inhabitants than has the far-away nation that rules it.

Manhood, a conscious recognition of the power that one inherently possesses, is the only safeguard to liberty. It is the only possession that gives a man freedom—freedom not only from the tyranny of another, but freedom from destructive vices, freedom from sickness, freedom from pitiful bondage to negative thoughts and moods. Say what we will, the strong ever rule the weak. A negative goodness is no protection whatever. The man that yields unresistingly to his own weakness, to the entreaties of others, and to untoward circumstances lacks manhood, and is far from the freedom that makes one a man in the true sense of the word.

He who has conserved his strength, who has not allowed false ideas to turn his natural desires into unnatural channels, who holds to a philosophy or a religion that is strong, virile, and full of love, but, withal, full of power and a sense of right—he is the man that is well-nigh invincible. Just as it is with the individual, so is it with the nation.

It is manhood of this type that the New Commandment teaches—manhood that results from a system of natural and rational living, which frees the body from weakness and disease, which strengthens and brightens the mind, which furnishes a natural religion, a religion that has for its theme the soul, the Divine Spark within, prototype of the Father, capable of being brought into conscious individuality and into a potency that is Godlike and all powerful. A system of natural living, three-fold in its application, including mind, body, and soul, will make of man a true Man, will give him the strength and the power and the goodness that enable him to resist all undesirable forces, be what they may, which would bind him to serfdom and cause him to do what he does not want to do or which would take from him something he truly loves.

It is men of this type—men who follow a system of rational living, men who give heed to the New Commandment — that will gradually free the world of its weaknesses, crimes, vices, and slavery. Weakness, crime, vice, and slavery are the result of destructive doctrines, doctrines that teach beggarism, a negative goodness, and the stagnation of desires and forces natural to man. As a result of destructive teachings, man no longer knows what is good and pure, and no longer cares whether men live or die, so long as he has reason to expect a heaven of bliss in the Hereafter.

As a result of such teachings, man is indifferent to everything except the one anticipation of bliss in the Hereafter, as a reward for denying himself physical pleasures and enjoyments in the here and now. He cherishes this anticipation, notwithstanding the fact that he has put forth no effort whatever to build a spiritual body, which will enable him to enjoy bliss in the Beyond.

This has been the history of nations: whenever a nation has given up positive goodness, that is, belief in the necessity of strong, virile manhood, and the necessity of bringing into perfection the powers of the physical being, as well as the soul, belief in the necessity of developing and unfolding the constructive and creative powers of his own nature, and belief in a virile religion—then that nation has begun to decline and decay.

Here, again, we have no better example than India, with its teeming millions; for it is in India, above all other countries, that we find negative goodness. In the main, India is a nation that holds to negative Yogism, which is a system of negative beliefs, negative goodness, and negative individualism. Religion of this type considers it a glorious thing for a man to deny all natural desires. This type of religion maintains that the chief end of man is to allow every natural desire and impulse to stagnate, and that desire for earthly possessions, earthly joy, earthly love, is a mortal sin, which denies the soul admittance into the realms of bliss. It may even go to the extreme of teaching that to sit in one posture until the body becomes stiff, to repeat certain prayers, to beg for a living, having neither houses nor lands nor place to lay the head, is the divine life.

It may be freely admitted that this class of religionists are not guilty of pronounced sins of commission. In their acts, in their conduct, in their life, may be manifest no grievous sin or evil. But theirs is constantly the sin of omission. Theirs is the sin of negativeness. Theirs is the sin of inactivity, of inertness, of weakness. They are guilty of the sin of non-effort to develop and to use the divine powers entrusted to them; consequently, through non-use, these powers wither and die, losing the possibility of becoming the instruments of conscious individuality. They perform no useful labor, thereby breaking the first and greatest command of God—which is, that man, being born in the image of the Creator, should be like Him. The Creator is truly and indisputably a God of activity, a Being of creative skill and power. In this respect in particular, man should be like his Creator— ever active, progressive, and alert.

Moreover, through this negative life, they crush out all strength and virility, that which is the glory of the true man. Through the weakness thus induced they either ignore or wilfully transgress the laws of nature, and eventually become slaves not only to themselves and their own false conception of life, but to others as well. For, in every land and in every age and in every clime, the stronger rules the weaker.

Of all nations, those of northern climates are the strongest. With few exceptions, the people of the north have believed in a God of activity, a God that takes delight in accomplishments, in new creations, in evolutions and developments and growth. Innately they feel that strength comes to man by doing that which falls to his lot to do.

Belief that earthly desires are wrong, belief in the subjection of the body—that these beliefs are necessary in order to make the soul fit for entrance into the kingdom of heaven, is the direct cause of weakness; and weakness is ever the cause of serfdom. He who is weak becomes the slave of weakness, a slave to his own wrong conception of life, first of all, then, a slave to others. A wrong conception of life is the cause of disease. They who believe that it is necessary for the body to suffer and to be in misery in order that the soul may be glorified, will naturally make no effort to strengthen the body; for, to do so would be sin. But physical weakness is not the end. It is rather the beginning of decline. In the beginning, the progenitors may be merely physically weak. Physical weakness, however, spreads and makes rapid inroads through the entire being of succeeding generations, until, in time, the people has become a nation of weaklings—weaklings in body, in mind, and in soul.

The inactive, effortless life causes the physical frame to weaken and to become disease-racked. This state gradually brings on mental weakness and disorders. Thus, the mind loses its accuracy in viewing things. Conditions of life are seen from a wrong angle and in an untrue perspective. That which, to the normal, healthy mind, is holy and worthy becomes to the morbid mind unholy and altogether undesirable, something, indeed, to be shunned. To a mind thus warped and distorted, every manly sport, everything in life that would help to build up the body, becomes a sin, something to be guarded against, to be condemned, possibly to be legislated against, until, in the end, there is only weakness and imbecility left. Such a state of weakness and negativeness will gradually unfit man for all that makes life worth the living. Such men become unfit for business. Even if they enter the legitimate marts of trade, they are dull and slow-witted, and are left far behind by their more active competitors.

The result is easily foreseen. Not being able to accummulate the necessities of life, they are unable to live respectably. Then, the morbid mind begins to ferment its deadly poisons. The mind so disordered through unnatural living and unnatural thinking is unable to determine the cause of its difficulties and to place the blame and the responsibility where they belong. Such a mind accuses others of unjust dealings and all other sins of which the human heart is capable. Such a mind blames others and places upon other shoulders the responsibility that properly belongs upon its own. The acceptance of a natural religion, a natural philosophy of life, a rational system of constructive living, would reveal to such a mind the cause of its difficulties and would enable it to remove the cause and to plant in its place the cause of better conditions.

It must be granted, on the other hand, that exploitation of the weak is by far too nearly universal. This is freely admitted. But the fact remains that no man need continue a weakling, that all men can gain a reasonable degree of physical strength and mental vigor, and thereby be able to cope with others, with those who would despoil them. All may gain sufficient strength and self-reliance to prevent others from despoiling him and his.

The world is sadly in need of men—men free from weakness, free from slavery to their own unnatural beliefs, and free from worship at the shrine of their own unnatural and destructive law. Sad, indeed, to think that the masses are in bondage to themselves and therefore to others!

The man that is clean and pure physically, mentally, and spiritually will have the advantage every time over the man that is physically and mentally and spiritually unclean and impure. The man who is truly man, physically, mentally, and spiritually, can be the slave of no one, not even of the most corrupt politician; for, just as the beast in the jungle knows when it meets a master, so the most degraded, though seemingly possessed of unlimited power, recognizes the superiority of him who manifests true manhood and true strength. In proportion as men recognize these facts and begin to live in harmony with them, those who now take advantage of the weak will be forced to give way and to relinquish their hold upon them. Then will be a brighter day.

The greatest degradation that a nation can know is when the men of that nation have sunk so low, through unnatural living and abnormal thinking, that they allow the few to deal unjustly with their women and children in whatever way they wish. Is there a lower stage to which

a nation can fall? Can there be anything more degrading than that the innocent should be exploited, injured, worked to death, starved to death, given no opportunity whatever for development either mental or physical?

Men are to be held accountable for their weakness because they have the opportunity to develop their powers, to strengthen their weak points, to live a natural life, and thus to become strong, virile, and free. But women and children are dependent on men for their protection, and where there is no manhood, then is there is no protection. Where there is no manhood, there is no conscience to call a halt; and the few in power without any moral sense whatever will drive the innocent to the farthest limit of work and torture.

And, in this instance again, India may be cited as an example—India, with its negative philosophy, with its negative teachings, that normal manhood, normal desires, desires for earthly happiness and joy, are destructive to the soul and will deny it entrance into the realms of bliss. Nowhere in all the world are the women and the children reduced to such a state of degradation as in far India with its once glorious, beautiful, and sublime philosophy.

The more of an imbecile a man becomes, the more ready is he to decry all that is manly. The more a slave to his own weakness he becomes, the more is he ready to blame others with his condition. The working man who is not earning a respectable living for his family is ready to decry those who give him employment. It is very probable that his employers do not treat him justly. This may be readily admitted. Nevertheless, it must be admitted, also, that this same man is unwilling to study and to apply himself and to put forth untiring effort to fit himself for better conditions. He is not willing to live a normal, natural life, in order to gain physical health and strength and the ability to think consecutively and con-

structively. He puts forth little effort to become so strong
that he need not be at the beck and call of the shrewd
and wiley. He does not truly seek freedom for himself
and for those he loves. He lives only to denounce and
to be exploited.

Let man begin to live the natural, normal life. Let
him give up those things which are unnatural, abnormal,
and weakening. Let him take up the constructive life.
Let him cultivate his mind and mental powers. Even
though he has but a few minutes each day to devote to
self-improvement, things will soon change, if he will only
make the best possible use of these precious moments.
The man who does this will soon be able to think and to
act for himself. He will act as he thinks in spite of un-
favorable circumstances. Such a man will soon be able
by his own manliness to prevent unjust dealings on the
part of others.

Let man seek his God. To do this is the eternal quest
of life. Yet let it be remembered that the quest for God
and the spiritual life is not the whole, but only the half,
of the true life. The other half is his duty to humanity
in general and to himself, in his threefold nature, body,
mind, and soul. Let him free himself, first of all, from
physical weakness and from physical defects; for, just as
long as there are physical abnormalities, so long will there
be mental deficiencies. So long as there are physical and
mental abnormalities and indiscretions, the soul cannot
reach perfection.

The tree on which the rose grows must be of good
stock. Otherwise, the rose cannot be perfect. Moreover, unless the sun shines upon the tree and the buds,
the rose cannot be perfect. The shadows grow, not beautiful flowers, but poisonous fungi.

In like manner, if the body of man is not brought to
a state of strength, the soul, which is the flower thereof,

cannot be perfect. The sunshine necessary to bring the blossom to perfection is the joy of life, the healthy desire for happiness, and love for one's fellow men.

The New Commandment, "Be a man and thou mayst be a god," is a religion of Manhood, of Godhood, of Freedom—freedom from every form and description of slavery because it is freedom from every form and description of weakness.

CHAPTER NINE

Natural Instincts Are the Promptings of Nature—the Handmaid of God, and the Mother of Goodness— and Are, Therefore, Good.

Natural instincts are given man for a noble purpose. In the normal man of a fair degree of health, natural instincts are the promptings of Mother Nature, telling him what to do and urging him to do it.

In the human heart, there are two sets of emotions. One set is the natural instincts, which have to do with the body and the physical being, its welfare and happiness. The other is from the Divine Being within the physical. This emotion is made known through the Voice of Conscience, or Intuition.

In the normal man, the physical part is co-equal with the soulual part of his nature. Neither one is greater than the other. If there is a preponderance of one over the other, the life of that man is, to that extent, abnormal and unbalanced, and is in need of a readjustment that will restore equilibrium.

The Voice of the physical being is natural instinct. The Voice of the soul is Conscience, or Intuition. The New Commandment, which admonishes the cultivation of manhood in order that Godhood may be realized, places equal stress on the importance of understanding and giving heed to each voice.

Those philosophies which teach that Nature herself is the antagonist of God, and that to follow Nature is to reap condemnation, also teach that natural instincts are evil and will lead to destruction of soul and to the forfeiture of a place in the heaven of peace. This is only to be expected. The latter is the logical conclusion of the former principle. If it be true that Nature is antagonistic to goodness, then it follows as an inevitable result that man's natural instincts are misleading. The New Commandment, however, with its emphasis upon manhood, virility, and activity, takes exception to the first premise, and distinctly teaches that Nature, the Handmaid of God, is good, and that man's natural instincts are inherently good. True, his instincts and impulses may become perverted, as, indeed, any good may be turned into wrong channels and thus become other than good. The doctrine that Nature is antagonistic to God and to goodness is part and parcel of an unnatural, negative, destructive philosophy. It has no place in the religion and the philosophy of him who is normal and well balanced.

Possibly the whole misconception has come about gradually through a misunderstanding of what is actually wrong and what actually constitutes sin. Time was when the falling in love of a young man with a fair maiden, if not agreeable to the parents of one or the other, was labelled witchcraft. The fact that a normal, vigorous, strong young man should become infatuated with the smile and the charms of a maiden, contrary to the parents' wishes, could be explained in no other way than that she was the messenger of the evil one, a witch, and that the boy innocently but unfortunately became the victim of her bewitching power. Strange idea this! So it seems to us now. Strange indeed, that any such interpretation could ever have been placed upon the normal, natural event of loving and being loved. Yet it is a simple item of history, that many have met a horrible death because they dared to follow the laws of God and of Nature and to cherish in the heart the most holy of all passions.

This one illustration serves as a sample of the many

misconceptions of right and wrong prevalent among men.
The discarded belief in witchcraft and the pitiful re-
strain, exacted upon the joyous spontaneity of childhood
are relics of the negative teachings of a past age. None
the less woeful and none the less disastrous, however,
are the negative doctrines of the present age and the
grievous misconceptions of right and wrong that have
grown out of them.

Fundamental among these negative teachings is the
erroneous principle that Nature and God are antagonistic terms and that natural instincts in man are antagonistic to the spiritual instincts of his nature. This principle inevitably leads to the conclusion that every natural
instinct and desire is wrong, and, consequently, to be
shunned. Love of home, friends, congenial surround-
ings; interest in temporal treasures and material con-
cerns; regard for the many possibilities of culture and
self-improvement; fondness for the artistic and the beautiful in every department of life—under the ban placed
upon natural instincts, all these normal inclinations of
the human heart are to be regarded as wrong! No wonder inertness and sluggishness become the pronounced
traits of him who accepts such a principle. No wonder
an entirely perverted and distorted view of life becomes
his who endeavors to carry out a principle like this.

In view of the fact that this negative doctrine, in
many subtle ways, is making inroads upon the people, the
time is ripe for marked emphasis to be placed upon the
New Commandment, "Be a man and thou mayst become a
god."

Manhood—virile, vigorous, strong, self-reliant, self-
assertive manhood—is the need of the hour. Manhood,
strength of character, activity, progress, advancement,
growth, power, virility, usefulness, and hearty co-operation in matters that concern the public weal—this must

be the ideal of him who aspires to Godhood and the Deific Consciousness.

Individuality—development of the manifold powers inherent, yet, for the most part, latent, in man's nature, and the employment of these powers in channels of useful endeavor—this ideal, the ideal of Individuality and negative goodness.

Let the watchword of the New Commandment—Manhood, must supplant the standard of inactivity and MANHOOD—be made to ring incessantly in the ears of men.

Let each honest heart become convinced of the goodness of Mother Nature. Let each realize that Nature is the Handmaid of God, His helper, aye, even His Spouse, honored and well beloved in His sight.

Let this truth be heralded far and near:

The natural instincts of the normal man represent the voice of Nature; and, if honored and obeyed by him, they become the means of leading him to his divine inheritance. They are stepping stones to the Deific Consciousness. Like anything else, they may be misunderstood, misapplied, misdirected, and even perverted. But, if correctly understood and normally satisfied, they are interpreters of truth, promoters of the highest good, and messengers of the Divine. The principle of interpretation to be applied to the instincts that prompt action is simple—namely, Will gratification of an impulse harm either the self or another? If so, gratification is forbidden. If not, it is granted. If gratification will harm or in any way weaken the self or bring sorrow, loss, or disadvantage to another, it is to be avoided, no matter how the impulse comes, whether as a natural instinct or as a cherished dogma of some religious sect.

Nature is the Mother of creation. Nature is the avenue through which God manifests. Just as it is necessary for the soul to possess a body through which to manifest its activities and to work out its destiny, so is Nature the channel through which God constantly manifests His creative functioning. Similarly, the natural instincts in man are the normal prompting of Nature, leading him to develop and to make the most of his divine powers, and thus to manifest his own God-likeness.

The origin of negative philosophies is worthy of comment. Every religious belief that has given to the world the idea that desire for earthly happiness, earthly love, and earthly possessions is evil, and that gratification of natural instincts is evil, was formulated by men of abnormal tendencies and abnormal habits. Either they had in youth gratified all instincts of their nature, natural and unnatural indiscriminately, or they were born with blighted natures. They may have been born with strong natural powers, which they abused to the utmost limit or they may have been born with a deficiency of natural powers. In either case, they were abnormal and unnatural. Thus, it is merely an historic fact, which may be verified by any earnest student, that the founders of negative doctrines have been men of abnormal, negative tendencies. The record of the founders should be sufficient to teach us what to accept and what to reject.

To remember the following facts will enable us to view Nature and natural instincts in a correct perspective. The force that gives natural instincts to man is the very force that causes the rose to spring up and grow, to put forth buds, which, with the help of the sun, burst open in glory into a perfect blossom. The force in nature that causes the lily to spring up from the soil, possibly a soil of mire and filth heavily polluted, is the very force that, in man, prompts him to love and be loved, to serve and be served, to enjoy and take delight in objects of grace and beauty. The lily, an emblem of absolute purity, as the rose, emblem of absolute perfection, fulfils its mission to the glory of God and Nature.

There is this difference between the force that opens the bud and ripens the fruit and the force that impels man to love, enjoy and take delight. Neither the rose nor the lily has free-will. They are each perfect recipients of the forces of nature that promotes growth. With man, however, it is different. Having the right of choice, he is not a perfect recipient of the law of goodness. He is not a perfect instrument through which the Law may function and manifest its beauty. Exercising the power of choice, he too often accepts an abnormal doctrine of life and thus turns into devious channels the law of Nature operating through him. He too often lives an unnatural, abnormal life, and does not even allow the physical being—the tree—to develop normal proportions. Much less does the flower—the soul within—under such conditions blossom into glory and beauty. In almost all instances, the plantlet, which might become the soul, is buried beneath a vast accumulation of rubbish—false beliefs, false conceptions, and perverse, detrimental habits of life. The Divine Spark within—the soul in process of making —does not even reach the bud state, much less the stage of the full blown rose, the stage of Illumination and Godhood.

In her domain, Nature is as absolute as is God in His domain. The physical side of existence belongs to Nature; to God, the spiritual side of being. Neither God nor Nature is false to the domain allotted to each. It is only man, although he incorporates in his being both God and Nature, who abuses his powers and dishonors both God and Nature. To abuse either his physical or his spiritual powers is to abuse and to dishonor both sides of his being.

He who refuses to respect and to obey the voice of

Nature made known to him through the normal instincts, fails to develop the physical being to its highest state of development. More than this, through neglect to perfect the physical, the spiritual suffers. The physical corresponds to the tree on which the rose grows, the stalk on which the lily blooms. Unless the tree and the stalk are strong and vigorous and thrifty, the rose and the lily cannot be perfect blossoms.

Natural instincts must teach man to be spontaneous and to live the normal, healthful life. The babe in the cradle is a specimen of wholesome spontaneity. The child, before it has developed self-consciousness and become hampered by the unnatural restraints demanded by an unnatural standard of life, is a sample of naturalness and ease. Almost the first expression of the babe is the smile. The smile represents joy and pleasantry. It represents a nature that is innately and instinctively joyous and free. This, the child nature, gives us the correct standard of life, and indicates that the natural instincts encourage and stimulate and foster joy, happiness, spontaneity, and naturalness.

With the normal, healthy child, the first requisite is physical satisfaction. For this, it expresses appreciation by the smile and other baby ways of showing peace and contentment. Through the body, the soul smiles its satisfaction and ease. As the child grows, in each stage of advance, it manifests in varying ways an inclination toward activity, pleasantry, and physical gratification. The healthy child unquestioningly heeds its natural promptings. It is satisfied with nothing less than almost incessant motion. It is forever doing something. In its enjoyment of play, everything else is forgotten.

This, however, is before the child has been taught a false philosophy, before he has been led to exercise abnormal restraint over his natural instincts and desires.

The stage of freedom and naturalness in the child gives way when he is led to question and to doubt the rightness of Nature's promptings. Under the false instruction that natural instincts are destructive and that desire for earthly pleasures and earthly joy interferes with man's eternal bliss, fear and restraint all too soon supplant ease, naturalness, and spontaneity.

If man were normal, he would do as the child does. He would satisfy the physical being with wholesome foods, the foods that sustain strength and vigor, the foods that properly nourish physical cravings, without unduly stimulating them. Like the child, he would bend all his energies into channels of creative work, creative and constructive thought, wholesome enterprises for the betterment of himself and others. With this, his natural instincts would be so thoroughly satisfied that they would not seek gratification in undesirable channels.

The philosophy that teaches man to repress natural instincts and to deny the desire for earthly joy and happiness, for the sake of gaining heavenly joy and bliss, succeeds in doing for heavenly joy the very thing it does for earthly joy and peace. To deny the one is to deny the other. Man is a twofold being with a twofold nature and a twofold duty. Consequently, he must live a twofold life. The life of the physical demands activity. The life of the soul finds satisfaction in a religious worship that stimulates and fosters daily development of soul powers. The soul is satisfied with nothing less than constant growth and progress. This demands activity, effort, and untiring zeal.

Some one may say that the New Commandment, in the honor it bestows upon Nature, encourages Nature Worship, that it takes man away from God, that it gives loose reins to the gross passions. Nothing can be farther from the truth. The New Commandment advocates normal gratification of normal instincts, natural gratification of natural instincts. By no means does it advocate indiscriminate indulgence. It recognizes that the desires and instincts of him who lives an unnatural, abnormal, inactive life are abnormal and unnatural. It recognizes that suppression of normal desires gives place to abnormal passions and vice, but that he who suppresses normal desires fails to see that which takes their place as something abnormal and degrading, because his judgment and his vision have become enslaved, weakened, and even poisoned through the impoverishment of suppressed desire.

Nature pays no homage to sorrow. The worship of sorrow has no part in the teachings of Nature or of God.

It must be admitted that he who has attained even the highest state of physical and spiritual development may experience sorrow, the loss of a friend or a loved one. He may experience loss of property or possessions. He may experience temporary defeat in a cherished plan. But, to him of lofty development of body and soul, it is not a "sorrow unto despair." To him, there may be the pain of parting; but he sees it only as a temporary loss. He sees all things as being in the process of change. Anything that is truly ours is ours forever, though it may undergo many and varied changes.

Wisdom is not something to lay hold of and to know, and to keep or to part with. Wisdom is a state of being into which we must grow, through obedience to both natural and divine law. Say what we will, man cannot fully and truly obey the Divine Law, while refusing obedience to the natural law. From one point of view, the two are twain. From another point of view, the two are one; and one is as important and as truly fundamental in its significance as the other.

If things of the soul alone are all-sufficient for man, it was an unwise plan for the Almighty Father to send the soul into the earth existence to gain experience and knowledge. Moreover, it seems little short of criminal on His part, to have planted in man's nature instincts and inclinations that are inherently evil, simply for the sake of testing his ability to deny them.

We are told that, when God created man, He looked upon His handiwork and pronounced it not only "good," but even *"very good."* Man was then innately and inherently as he is now—endowed with divine attributes and potentialities and possibilities. He possessed the instincts and the cravings that belong to a natural being in a natural world. He couched in his being the Divine Spark, then as now—the spark of Divinity within his humanity, capable of becoming an individualized center of Deific Consciousness. There is this difference, however: on the day of creation as referred to in the Biblical narrative, man was in a world ruled by Nature, the Handmaid, the Bride, of God, and not, as now, in a world hampered and oppressed by the rule of false, unnatural, negative philosophies.

Before man can become natural (and he must become natural before he can become divine), it is necessary for him to cast aside, and to throw into the limbo of forgotten things, the belief that natural instincts are destructive and degrading. He must accept a new philosophy, the New Commandment, which teaches that the natural is the means by which, and through which, he is to reach the Divine. He must cease repressing normal instincts. He must rather see that they are properly cultivated and given every opportunity to expand into natural powers. The natural instinct that is satisfied in a normal way becomes a natural power. Every available power must be used in the development of divine strength and in the building of a foundation whereon a mighty soul, the Divine Being, the Son of God, may be erected.

It is impossible to know peace, joy, happiness, and contentment in the world to come unless one lays the foundation for it here and now. In order to find its completeness in the next state of existence, one must find its beginning here and now. To honor Nature and Nature's Voice in the human breast, is as important as to honor Nature's God.

CHAPTER TEN

To the weak, a doctrine of weakness seems natural

Man can understand only those things which he himself is capable of doing. The things that others do, which he cannot do, are to him a closed book. When one who has reached old age sees others perform feats that require great strength and close application of body and mind, he wonders how it can be done. He even looks back upon his own earlier achievements and marvels at the thought of having performed them.

For this reason—that man cannot comprehend anything of which he himself is incapable of experiencing—wisdom cannot be taught man through a mere external process of acquirement. Man must grow into the condition or the state that makes wisdom possible. Wisdom is the result of ripened experience. He who solves a problem, passing carefully through every step of its solution, understands how it is done. He who has benefitted by various experiences in life and has laid up a fund of valuable information understands how wisdom comes. He understands how to estimate the price of wisdom. The ignorant and the inexperienced understand neither the price nor the value of wisdom.

Similarly, only the strong understand the possibility of strength. To the weak, strength is a mystery. Only he who forgives, can comprehend the marvels of a forgiving spirit. He who forgives not, cannot comprehend that it is possible for God to be a forgiving Being. He who loves not, cannot comprehend that it is possible for God to be a Being of Love. To the impotent, virile manhood seems unnatural, even something to be feared, or avoided, even condemned. He who does not possess strength beholds strength as an object of pity. The weak, whether their weakness is moral or physical, consider their state preferable to that of strength. They mistake weakness for humility, and count it a God-sanctioned virtue.

A glance at the sports sanctioned and encouraged by a nation indicates much concerning the character of that nation. If the national sports are calculated to develop strength and valor, courage and prowess, physical perfection is reflected in the character of the people. This is the case among peoples that cherish the ideal of virility and activity, force and power. Among peoples with whom the doctrine of quietism holds sway, the favorite sports are of the feminine type, requiring little exertion. Their habits tend toward asceticism. Their games and pastimes call for meager outlay of strength and skill. Again, peoples who incline toward asceticism are ever ready to condemn the manly sports of those nations which honor physical strength and endurance. A race that has lost its strength and virility is sure to adopt a philosophy or a creed that has its foundation in human weakness. In its inert, effeminate state, it is sure to be attracted by a doctrine that denies the good and the manly, a doctrine that condemns earthly joy, peace, happiness, and earthly possessions.

Physical weakness and a negative creed go hand in hand. Physical strength and powerful mentality and wholesome morality go hand in hand with a constructive, positive philosophy or religion. In the Northland, where existence itself demands remarkable physical endurance, the Viking religion has flourished. In the Viking religion, there is no such thing as fear. The coward is placed lower in the scale of being than is the cur on the street, and has little more chance of living. In the East, continually warmed by the rays of the sun, where shelter and clothing are items of small consequence, where little food is required—and that such as nature provides—where there is no necessity for the display of strength and valor, where self-exertion is not necessary in order to meet the needs of existence, we find a nation whose religion and philosophy correspond to the character of the people. No wonder that, in the warm clime of the Orient, a philosophy flourishes that makes inertness its chief glory. No wonder that constructive thought, desire for better things, useful labor, manly pastimes, are wanting. No wonder that we find here a race whose religious belief and philosophy are held sacred because of the very fact that no self-exertion, no manhood, no effort whatever, are required to live them.

That in life which requires no effort to live, no self-exertion, no self-dependence and self-reliance, will give no strength. In fact, it will result in additional weakness. In spite of this fact, aye, possibly for this very reason, a philosophy of ease, inactivity, and passivity is readily accepted by the multitudes. Their own indifference and fondness of ease make them an easy prey to a doctrine that honors meek, unquestioning acceptance of so-called authoritative dogma. Nor do they comprehend that weakness is being added to weakness. That which requires little effort is attractive to the average man; for the average man loves idleness and listlessness more than strength and activity. Implicit acceptance of ideas worked out by others has a seductive charm for him who is too indolent to think for himself.

From these considerations, it can readily be seen why the New Commandment is being brought forcibly before the public mind. There is a reason for it. There is need of it.

"Be a Man, and thou mayst become a god."

The doctrine of Manhood and ultimate Godhood requires effort on the part of him who accepts it. Effort is required in the accomplishment of worthy objects in life. Effort and self-assertiveness, exertion and self-reliance and self-mastery must supplant every form of weak passivity and inertness. The New Commandment sanctions effort, and an active, whole-souled participation in all things that claim one's attention. In its sports, in its enjoyments, in its possessions, in its pleasures, in its achievements, in its daily labor and routine tasks, the New Commandment honors vim, courage, and an active, whole-hearted coopera- tion with others. With every effort will come a correspond- ing degree of power. Every effort accumulates added strength with which to put forth added effort. Through constant accumulation and enjoyment of power man be- comes super-man. And, in the very joy of living, he is repaid an hundred fold for every effort made.

The man without power, without possessions, is a non-influential man. This is an observation that cannot be contradicted. It is indeed a fundamental law. Take for example the man that lives a passive life, though free from evil. He begins the day with thoughts free from censure and injury to others. He gives his time during the day to the work at hand, such amount as is necessary. He makes no active effort to accomplish any great thing, nor to gain possession of more than he actually needs, though more is his due. He may be good and noble at heart, but, through indifference to larger interests, he fails to gain influence among men. So far as it goes, the life of such a man is not to be condemned. But let a question of grave importance arise in his neighborhood, a question that involves the good of vast numbers; and, when it comes to exercising influence in regard to settling the question, it is found that this man cannot turn a single vote in favor of the right. His life has been comparative- ly upright and harmless, but not powerful for good among men. Then, again, he who lives an upright, harmless life among others, but does not avail himself of the opportunity to accumulate gain, is not in a position to help an unfortunate brother in time of need or help on a worthy cause, which may be struggling to attain a place of greater usefulness among men. Surely, it is a laudable ambition to desire power, influence, and earthly possessions for the sake of the good one may do therewith in worthy enterprises.

Negative goodness is a weakness, though possibly not so great a weakness as negativeness without goodness. The one who lives a life not altogether free from evil may be the means of doing greater good to a greater number of people than the one who lives a negatively good life. This, for the reason that he who has gained power and influence, though his life may not be absolutely above reproach, is in a position to use his power and his influence for good in such a way as to set into motion that which will bring great good to a great number.

Weakness is of many types. The righteous man may be as guilty of weakness as is the unrighteous man. Though he may be living a blameless life so far as standards of moral conduct are concerned, yet, by not making use of his inherent potential powers, he is not ready to use power at a time when power is needed. In this case, he is held accountable for the inability to do that which he should have been able to do. He is guilty of non-development and non-use of potential power. We are indeed held responsible for the inherent powers with which we are endowed. Neglect in the cultivation and the use of talents entrusted to us is indeed a grievous weakness. Indifference to the opportunities presented to us for helping a noble and worthy cause which demands an enormous outlay of money in order to spread its blessings among vast numbers—this, too, is a weakness. Indeed, passivity, negativeness, and indifference in any form are to be classed as weakness.

Through a strange fallacy of appearances, the life a man lives gives color to his beliefs, and causes any other type of life to seem abnormal, unnatural, and undesirable. To the weak, a doctrine of weakness seems perfectly natural. Consequently, the mind must be set free from its self-thought and its self-content and its narrow-mindedness before it is ready to accept a doctrine that exalts strength, helpfulness to others, and a courageous, manly spirit. Strange though it may seem, to the man who, through a certain course of living, has become a weakling, the outlook of life has completely changed; and that which to the normal, healthy mind is right and proper, as, for instance, deeds of valor and of honor, to the weakling are something to be condemned.

Thus it is that, to the weakling, life itself is a delusion and a snare, something to become free from as soon as possible. Those things, then, which tend to weaken the hold of the earthly life upon us are to be welcomed. To him who has become enamoured by negative doctrines, the greatest delusion is the belief that weakness and sickliness of body will result in greatness of soul, and will give man a *"Carte Blanche"* to the heaven of bliss.

A line of demarkation must be drawn in respect to weakness that cannot be helped and weakness that can be helped. For instance, it is often the case that the person born a cripple or blind or bereft of other of the natural senses becomes a woman or a man of power, of honor, of clear-sightedness, of superior ability in some particular direction, and even a mighty leader among men. It is to be noted, however, that these do not worship weakness in any form. Nor do they attain greatness *because of their handicapped condition, but in spite of it.* They understand full well that weakness is undesirable. Consequently, they set about to bring into play every atom of power in their natures in order to rise above their limitation. Even in their present state, they become giants. Yet who can say how much more they might have accomplished with all their powers, had they used the same amount of perseverance. Of these, too much cannot be said in praise; for, handicapped apparently from birth, they have, nevertheless, accomplished wonders and arisen almost to the state of super-men.

Any chiding that the New Commandment may have, is for those who are favorably born and favorably conditioned, but who, through inertness and an effortless existence, have lapsed into weakness and indifference. Chiding is for those, who, not satisfied with a life of physical, mental, and spiritual impotence, even teach a doctrine of impotence and find a ready market for their teachings. The New Commandment aims not at the easiest doctrine, but at the best. A doctrine of ease and inactivity may at first seem easy and attractive; but, in the end, it proves to be the galling yoke of bondage. The doctrine of manhood, effort, exertion, and self-assertiveness in ways of usefulness, at first seems hard; but, in the end, it proves to be the blessedness of Godhood and Supermanhood.

Earth is not a land of sorrow unless we allow it to become such through our own weakness and imbecility. Earth may be a garden of delight, a garden wherein grow all beautiful flowers and all precious herbs, wherein may be found peace, happiness, and joy. True, there are times when into the garden of life will creep things that are undesirable. But the master mind soon frees itself from these conditions. To such a mind, losses and misfortunes are only stepping stones to greater power. The final parting with friends is only an indication of change to better conditions for that friend, and is not something to mourn over; for the two will meet again and will be the happier and the wiser for the temporary parting and the new meeting.

Watch the movements of the healthy boy of ten. Is there anything in his nature or his conduct to indicate that life is undesirable? Does anything in his manner and ways suggest the desirability of becoming free from earthly existence? .Watch him in his play. Is there a thought of sorrow? Does the dark side of life cast a shadow over his spontaneity? To him, the mere thought of living is a joy. In the romp and frolic, there is joy. The simple tasks assigned him by a fond parent, the study outlined by a wise teacher, he hastens to finish, in his eagerness to return to the play that awaits him. Who would be so cruel as to throw the shadow of doubt and gloom over the spontaneity of childhood?

True, at times, a discordant note creeps in, as, for instance when there is punishment for disobedience or when he meets with one of greater strength who defeats his plans. But not for a moment does he "drop down and out," and think of life as something to be free from. Not in the least, he soon forgets and begins to enjoy some new adventure.

As with the boy, so with the healthy man. Life is both a playground and a school. There are hours for play, and these are to be fully enjoyed and improved. There is time for labor, and for strenuous effort. This he accepts with right good-will. This he welcomes as a test of capability, a test of strength. In time, he comes to regard the graver duties and heavier tasks as feats on the playground of life—feats of skill and dexterity, feats of valor and honor. Severe trials and crises which confront him, delays in his cherished plans, obstructions in the way and temporary annoyances—these, to the master mind, become gymnastic feats, which impel consecutive thought and constructive self-training. There is joy in surmounting obstacles, joy in overcoming difficulties—a joy superior to the joy of him who wins in a race. The more difficult and stupendous is an undertaking, the greater is the pleasure of accomplishment. These thoughts are goads, which stimulate effort and exertion, courage and incessant toil, in him who chooses manhood as the standard of life. Say what we will, there is no such thing as fail in life for us unless we admit that we cannot succeed. Failure is for the weak and the fearful. He who fears to try is already a failure.

At the root of all weakness is either ignorance of the laws of life or disobedience to them. It matters not what it is, the result is always the same and is to be discouraged. This is true of individuals and of nations. The parent or the nation that encourages youth in that type of sports and games which tests strength, courage, valor, and skill, will produce men of power. Their power comes neither through war nor through shrewdness, but through fitness to rule, through keenness of mind, through strength and endurance of body, and through proficiency in all affairs that concern the public weal.

In order to overcome moral weakness and its nearest of kin, an abnormal idea of life, it is necessary to gain physical health and vigor. This is necessary to a normal view of life, life both on this plane of existence and on the plane succeeding this. Free the system of disease and physical weakness and abnormalities, and you free the mind of ignoble, diseased, negative thought. Through right living and proper recreation, give the body health and strength, and you fill the mind with noble and worthy desires, noble and healthy instincts. This soon leads to the desire to be up and doing, the desire to accomplish, to achieve and to be. Eventually, such standards of life and thought create men who are more than mere men, even super-men.

The body that is diseased and distorted and disordered cannot have healthy imaginations. As is the imagination, so will be the philosophy or the standard of life. *As a man is, so he thinketh.* This is worthy of becoming a truism, equal, if not superior, to the saying of wisdom, "As a man thinketh, so is he."

The New Commandment is pronounced in its emphasis upon manhood, activity, naturalness, spontaneity, and the joy of existence. Those who promulgate the doctrine of manhood as the only pathway to Godhood see reasons for emphasizing a constructive, active, optimistic philosophy. They see reasons in abundance for sounding the alarm in regard to the subtle inroads of a negative, inert philosophy of life. For passivity and idleness, for ease and lethargy, they would substitute the standard of toil, usefulness, effort, self-exertion. For belief in the doctrine of *no-desire*, they would substitute the blessedness of *one supreme desire*, as an active force among lesser desires, which are subservient to the one supreme desire of one's life. In the place of the belief that natural instincts are harmful and therefore to be shunned, they would plant the idea that natural gratification of natural instincts is Nature's method of accumulating power which may be employed in self-betterment and betterment of the race. They would root out of the garden of life the poisonous belief that earthly joy and earthly possessions prevent heavenly joy and heavenly possessions. In its place, they would plant the ideal that earthly joy and earthly possessions, rightly used, are natural means, in a natural world, of gaining imperishable joys and imperishable treasures in a heavenly world.

Philosophy based on the New Commandment honors toil and work, planning and execution of ideas. It honors him who accumulates earthly possessions through legitimate means, not at the expense or injury of others, but through his own honest efforts and efficient service. Religion based on the New Commandment throbs with life and power in the estimate it places on the value of a human soul. It leads to development of soul and fills the soul with Divine Fire. It brings peace and contentment in the thought that, here and now, begins the life of Light and Love, so that that which is called death becomes merely the change of planes from the present life to future joy in a world of Light and Love.

CHAPTER ELEVEN

Total depravity comes only through living a depraved life.

A philosophy based on the New Commandment does not sanction the doctrine that man is born in sin or that, at birth, he is a totally depraved creature. That man is born with sin in his nature, is accepted as true by those who believe in the Law of Reincarnation. The doctrine of reincarnation is the only doctrine that attributes justice to both God and Man. Any other disposition makes of God a being of injustice. The principle of reincarnation, however, is very different from the doctrine of total depravity at birth.

The teaching that man is born in sin and through sin, comes from the Orient. But, in the process of being transplanted from eastern to western soil, it has been woefully distorted and perverted, and has utterly lost its significance as originally understood by sages of the rising sun.

According to the Eastern doctrine of reincarnation, the man who has lived on the earth, but has not fulfilled his destiny in freeing himself from evil and in bringing the Divine Spark, the soul, into full Illumination and Conscious Oneness with God, passing out in this imperfect condition, is given the opportunity to return to the earth again and again. Indeed, if he is earnestly striving to accomplish that for which the earth plane is designed, he is given the opportunity repeatedly, until he succeeds in freeing the soul from imperfections and in bringing it to a state of Divine Consciousness and Individuality. This is a doctrine of justice and of divine consideration for the welfare of man, each individual being placed on his own merits and treated accordingly. Whereas, the doctrine of total depravity makes all men wicked and depraved in nature to begin with, and offers them only the one lifetime for redeeming themselves from their wicked estate. Moreover, according to the doctrine of total depravity, this one-life opportunity necessitates that they must suffer eternal condemnation. From beginning to end, the doctrine of depravity is based on injustice and heartless compulsion. It is a libel on everything that is holy and divine and noble in man's nature.

According to the principle of reincarnation, when a child is born, he is either the covering of a new soul, or is necessarily a soul that has returned, and, for that very reason, is born with sin and imperfection in his nature, which must be overcome. Had he no sin and no imperfections, that is, were he perfect, he would not be returning to the earth. Only under very rare conditions, does a soul that has attained perfection return to the earth. Thus, generally speaking, the soul that returns to the earth is born with sin. This is a very different matter, however, from saying that it is born in sin. There is no sin in giving birth to the human race. It was the express command of God that woman should be fruitful, and it is the divine decree and wish that souls should be born on the earth; therefore, the fact of giving birth to souls on earth cannot, in itself, be accounted as sin. The Law of Reincarnation has been misquoted and misinterpreted; and the teaching that man is born in sin and it utterly depraved in nature has no foundation whatever.

Twin to the doctrine that man is born in sin is the perverse teaching that some are born utterly depraved. Nothing can be farther from the truth. If man so lives during a given earth life as totally to destroy the individuality, when he dies there is no opportunity given for him to return to the earth plane. The body, the physical being, returns to the earth elements whence it came. The Divine Spark, not awakened, but covered over with the rubbish of a perverted, depraved life, did not receive the stamp of individuality. Consequently, it returns to the storehouse of Him who gave it, possibly to be sent out again on its pilgrimage.

There is no question that total depravity is possible. It results, however, from a certain type of living on the earth plane. There is neither indication nor proof that man was born in a depraved state. Unnatural living is the cause of total depravity. Conscious, wilful, deliberate violation of the laws of nature and of God leads to total depravity. Ignorance of the truth, false beliefs, erroneous standards of life, are the beginnings of a destructive, negative career. These, in time, lead to deliberate or to unconscious violation of the Divine and Natural Law. Yet even this results in total depravity only as man gradually kills out all that is good in his nature. Whether violation of Divine Law is conscious or unconscious, the results are the same. If any difference, unconscious is more subtle and more insidious. It makes its inroads upon the nature more treacherously, blinds the eyes to the truth, dulls and blunts the senses; and, most serious of all, it so perverts one's vision of life as to make error seem truth, vice seem virtue.

In the creation of man, it was the divine intention that he should accomplish certain things in life. Nor was he left absolutely helpless in regard to determining what he should accomplish and how he should accomplish. He was endowed with an indicator by means of which he might know what and how. This indicator is in the form of natural desire. Natural desires and instincts are the indicators divinely given man for the purpose of guiding him and of giving him the inclination to do and to become. They indicate what a man has power to do and to become.

They show in what direction his power and his possibilities lie. They not only indicate possibilities, but they even become, through normal exercise, the accumulators of power. They are more than indicators and directors and guides. Even the means by which power is generated and accumulated are they. If man fails to heed the natural promptings given to him as indicators, he fails to develop the powers with which he is endowed. In this way he fails to fulfil his destiny. In this way, either his powers lie dormant or they break out as vices and destructive tendencies in other directions. If a man follows and heeds the natural promptings given him as directors and indicators, he thereby develops and stores up power which may be employed in useful avenues. The highest use for the power thus developed is in awakening his own soul to activity through a life of usefulness to others. Through keeping his powers in proper channels, he not only redeems his own soul of its imperfections, but, by the example and the inspiration of his life, he exercises a redeeming influence over others.

But, sad to say, in numberless cases, the child born with good health, a good constitution, strong desires and great capabilities, is taught a false doctrine from the very beginning of life. He is forced to repress and to suppress natural instincts. His spontaneity is checked. Things not wrong in themselves, but contrary to the ideas of those who have the child in control, are constantly forbidden. The repression of innocent desires and incentives converts them into a poison to the brain and the storehouse of powers within. The result is that harmless, natural instincts, through suppression, are turned into secret vices which grow and accumulate as time goes on. Instead of the child's being taught what to do and how to do, he is taught nothing at all except that this and the other he must not do. Every repression adds more fuel to the fire. Herein is the beginning of hiding desires and promptings under the false impression that they must be wrong for the very reason that he feels inclined to gratify them. This is the inception of total depravity.

The child, in truth, is born with sin, though not necessarily in sin. It is the duty of progenitors to keep a guard over the instincts and desires of childhood. But a thing of greater importance is that progenitors shall be able themselves to distinguish between constructive and destructive desires and instincts. So long, however, as men believe that natural instincts are evil, that the desire for joy and happiness is evil, that earthly possessions are a passport to condemnation, and that life itself is undesirable, the child is almost sure to reap gloom and doom, unless its nature is so strong and healthy that it cannot be perverted. It is often the case that the child is healthy enough to rise above environmental conditions, and, in young manhood or womanhood, is able to redeem that part of its nature which was perverted in childhood.

In the majority of instances, depravity in a child is to be traced directly to the parent. Usually, the parents have held to a false religious or philosophical belief or else they have paid no attention whatever to the child except to tell it to stop doing this or that, without supplying something to take the place of that which the child had been doing. Nothing is more important than that the child shall be kept busy. Depraved men and women result from ignorance of the Law that, in order to keep the child or the youth or the mature man and woman from doing wrong, we must keep him busy and fully occupied in doing the right. To make the child stop doing wrong is far from sufficient. It is of paramount importance, to supply it with something to do in the place of the wrong. It is wiser if possible to remove the cause of its wrong doing, without arousing questioning and suspicion on the part of the child.

In the place of the undesirable, give it something equally charming, equally desirable. To force a child to stop is to repress an inclination in the child. This repression acts as an incentive to something else. And the child soon learns to indulge secretly in the things that have been forbidden. In this is the beginning of wrong, the beginning of faults, which gradually develop into vices, and these into still greater vices.

There are two urges in human nature. These are especially strong in the child up to the age of responsibility. The urge of the Divine impels the child to do that which is right, that which is normal and healthy. There is also another urge which is prompted by the carnal life and the carnal desires. But, in the child up to the age of responsibility, the carnal nature is less pronounced than the divine nature. And the wise parent will see that the child has every opportunity to follow these inclinations which are normal and healthy and natural. Every child has these inclinations and these desires; and they will develop naturally unless repressed by the parent or those who fill a parent's place.

In the young, purity and naturalness are innate. These qualities are a part of the child-nature. Real depravity cannot begin in the child until the age of responsibility. True it is, that the seeds of depravity are sown and the conditions of error are created before this time; but the actual wrong, the actual evil, begins with the age of accountability. There is no such thing as natural depravity. At all times, in all ages, and in all climes, depravity is unnatural. In every human being, there are two natures, two inclinations. These are present even in the youngest child. But, in the very young child, it is the angelic side, the natural and the normal instinct, that rules the life. And, if the parent is wise, it is these inclinations and desires which will be cultivated. Gratification of these will bring into being other natural and normal desires; and, as these are satisfied rather than repressed, still other desires come to take their place, until, at last, the youth is ready for the age of responsibility. Under this type of development, there is little danger of his following the path of depravity, though, to be sure, it is possible, owing to later associations and environments.

There is one safe means of preventing a depraved or ill-chosen life: that is, for mankind to lay hold of a religion or a philosophy that is natural, normal, and divine. A safe doctrine teaches individual responsibility. It exalts selfhood and manhood. It spurns the doctrine that man is a worm of the dust, a depraved creature, a spawn of the earth. On the other hand, a safe doctrine guards against that type of bigotry and narrow-mindedness which prevents growth and self-betterment. A disagreeable self-satisfaction and self-glory have no place in the doctrine of individual responsibility. One may realize that we are placed on the earth for a purpose, with a grave responsibility, a mighty mission to perform, even with inherent deific powers at our disposal for development and use; yet this realization should be the means of stimulating effort and honest endeavor. There is no excuse for him who has a true philosophy of life to "rest on the oars" of ease and self-content. The doctrine of life that keeps one in the safe path of manhood and selfhood emphasizes the desirability of living. According to such a philosophy, it is our privilege, aye, even our duty, to seek happiness, to seek the joys of life; and to seek earthly possessions, as a means of attaining higher interests, is also seen to be a worthy aim. Instead of being wrong, it is highly desirable to seek the joys of natural living. Not a diseased body and a dwarfed soul, but a healthy body and an illumined soul, in short, Sonship with the Father, is the ultimate end of a safe and sane philosophy of life.

An understanding of the mighty commandment, "Be a Man, and thou mayst be a god," reveals our responsibility to childhood. We will encourage in the child those things which make for health and strength and true pleasure. We will discourage only those things which tend to make it weaker, or might result in injury, either physical, mental, or spiritual. That which injures one department of its threefold nature will affect harmfully the other departments. This kind of care will do much toward bringing perfection and salvation in later life.

The purpose in life may be summed up in one word— Transmutation, the changing of one thing for another. Man comes to earth and takes on a body through which to manifest. In the beginning, the body is highly material, and contains all the desires of the material. This material foundation is, in reality, the very thing that gives the possibility of experiencing joy, happiness, and peace. All the senses have a physical base. The ideal placed before man, however, is to lift his desires from the plane of the material to the plane of the spiritual. This is a process of trans. mutation, or change from the lower to the higher.

The duty of man on earth is to find those pleasures, those desires and actions, which will lift him from bondage to the material and the carnal, and will establish in his character love for that which is constructive and eternal in its nature. Any pleasure to the physical being that gives health and strength and is free from injurious effects upon mind and heart, is desirable and praiseworthy. Through the fact of strengthening the physical being, it also strengthens mind and soul.

That physical delights may have a beneficial effect on mind and soul is easily illustrated. Take for example the game of baseball. To him who enjoys the game, to him who holds an exalted standard of correct and fair playing, to him who has no inclination to indulge in unfair means, the game is stimulating to mind and soul, as well as body. There is nothing about the sport that is brutal or harmful or degrading to the sensibilities. But it is equally true that physical delights may be deleterious to mind and soul. Take, for instance, the pastime enjoyed in some countries, the bull fight. This is a sport that gives health and strength to the body. It is in fact a great developer of the physical being. But it is a degrading pastime, in that it stimulates love for blood and brutality. Its effects are destructive to both mind and soul. It is detrimental to the finer nature of man.

All things in life naturally fall into one of these two classes. The wise parent will substitute the good and the healthful and constructive pastimes for the bad, harmful, and destructive. This leads the child gradually to love only the good and the constructive.

Nature recognizes no such thing as total depravity. That which is depraved becomes so through its own choosing and through its own living. Depravity is the result of ignorance and of erroneous religious and philosophical teachings.

CHAPTER TWELVE

Health is necessary to the highest degree of manhood and of manliness.

Health and manliness form the basis of the laws of Moses. Throughout the Hebraic Scriptures, the necessity of obedience to the laws of health is clearly indicated. Companion to the laws of health is to be found the encouragement given to deeds of valor and of strength. Health and valorous deeds form the basis of morality.

Obedience to the laws of health in respect to all items that concern positive strength and freedom from disease is the foundation on which the New Commandment is based. For, without a reasonable degree of health and strength, the highest form of manhood and manliness is impossible.

Good health means a clear brain, the power to think clearly, concentratedly, and consecutively. Good health means normal, natural instincts. Who has ever known of a morbid mind in a strong vigorous body? Good health means wholesome, optimistic imaginations, and noble, lofty, worthy plans and ideals. It means stimulus to activity and constructive, creative work. It means vim, enterprise, and interest in things that concern the general good. But, where there is disease of body, where there is pain and disorder, thoughts and desires, and imaginations become unnatural and discordant; and unhealthy, morbid mental states affect the character, the heart and the soul.

The laws of Moses are the result of wisdom gained through varied experience. They are accordingly conclusive and reliable. In giving to mankind his counsel concerning health and sanitation, Moses had to deal with a class of men who lived much in the open air, amid conditions of freedom for the entire body. But he had previously become familiar with city life, where conditions at best are unnatural, where there is congestion, imperfect sanitation, and other items that tend to impair health. It was, therefore, long and varied experience that qualified Moses to impart wise counsel to his people. So wise, indeed, are his laws regarding health and freedom from disease and weakness that they are considered the basis of the best sanitary laws known to man today. The fact that a leader of men like Moses considered the body and its well-being of such vast importance, ought to be to us a strong argument in favor of careful observance of the laws of health.

Health is the foundation of all that is good and desirable. Indeed, impossible of successful contradiction is the assertion that there cannot be a high degree of peace, joy, and happiness in a body that is disease-racked and full of pain. Such a condition cannot help making the mind dwell on unwholesome subjects. Morbid thoughts soon result in morbid actions. Power and influence among others wane in proportion to the lassitude and the lethargy of the physical. On the other hand, the body that is full of health and strength generates a mighty force or power, called magnetism. Magnetism is simply good health radiating from the center of life. In the normal physical being, the center of life is so full of vital energy that it cannot contain within itself all the vitality generated. This surplus of life principle is in a state of constant radiation, a condition that makes the individual magnetic and attractive to others. Such an individual becomes a powerful influence. He is ever alert, animated, and full of interest in the affairs of life. His thoughts and imag-

inations are full of good cheer and hope. This very mental state attracts to him the desirable things of life.

Life in the country, amid natural conditions, is the
ideal. The city is a center of activity, a center of advantages in many ways. It is a fact, nevertheless, that
constant living in the city makes the highest efficiency impossible. This is due to many reasons. The fact of its
being of activity keeps it more or less in a state of congestion. There is no such thing as perfect quiet. Both
day and night, almost constantly, is heard the hum of industry and the noise of confusion. The highest degree of
strength and power demands peace and quietness during
sleep. It is during sleep that absorption of strength takes
place. If sleep is disturbed, absorption is interfered with;
and man does not accumulate the strength that he might
under other conditions. It is very true that man may come
to the point where noises apparently do not affect him.
He may retire to rest at night apparently oblivious to
all external conditions of confusion. The subconscious
mind, nevertheless, registers the impression; and rest is
not perfect. Consequently, the absorption of strength is
below normal.

Other reasons than the state of congestion and constant confusion make city life less conducive to the highest degree of physical and mental efficiency. In a thickly
populated city, the atmosphere is more or less tainted with
poisonous gases and vapors. It is a law of nature that
the exhalations of human life are inhaled by plant life,
and the exhalations of the plant kingdom are inhaled by
the human kingdom. Thus, in the country, there is a mu-
tual exchange between the human and the vegetable worlds
of a most wholesome kind. The air is kept purified, and
full of vitality and strength; and, above all, it is permeat-
ed with nature herself. In the city, where there is a scarc-
ity of trees, flowers, shrubs, grains, where there is noth-

ing but man and the manufacturing and mechantile interests of man and the effluvia therefrom, there is nothing to purify the atmosphere. Be the conditions ever so
fair, there is still meager opportunity for perfect cleans-
ing of the air.

Again, according to the testimony of statistics, the
disease ratio and the death ratio are greater in the city
than in the country. This is due to the constant mixing of
the personal magnetism of the thousands or the millions,
as the case may be. The intimate and uninterrupted confusion of personalities also accounts for the large percentage of crime and immorality found in congested sections
of cities. Many of the habits that hold sway in the city
do not flourish in the country. As, for example, the opium
habit flourishes in the city. Whereas, it is seldom that
one finds an opium fiend in the country. The air, impregnated with the life of the vegetable kingdom, makes it
almost impossible for one to be unnatural to the extent
necessary to become a slave to this drug. If, perchance,
one does become addicted to this habit, he does not long
remain in the country, but goes to the city where he finds
associations of his own status in life.

Once more, living in the country with nature and
working with nature develops individuality in men and
women. They come to think the thoughts of nature.
Through constant association with Mother Nature, they
come to think along harmonious lines. The effect of rural
environment is seen in the case of a business man who
seeks the country for a rest and a change. He soon becomes impregnated with the desire and the fervor of nature. The languor and the restraint of conventionality
soon give place to the consciousness of vitality and of new
interest in life. The rod and the line tempt him to the
favorite pastime of the farmer boy. The luscious fruits,
the fields of waving grain, the voices of the night, the balmy,

invigorating air, become a delight and a charm unequalled
by the artificial glamor of city walls and streets. Nor does
it end with mere delight. He is attracted in due time
even by the thought of labor itself. The hoe in the hand
gives more pleasure than the cigar in the mouth formerly
afforded. Ere he is aware, Nature has wrought a transformation in him. The process of passing from one state
to another has been so gradual and so natural that he
scarcely knows how it has come about. He bears the
stamp of individuality and dares to be a man as nature
intended him to be.

On the other hand, note the change wrought in the
man who is transplanted to the city. He may be free from
conspicuous vice and evil, yet he soon takes on the habits
of his new associates. The cigar, the liquor, the language,
the characteristic gait, gradually, the restlessness, of the
city become his acquisitions. Life in the city being unnatural, his thoughts and mental state soon become tainted. Congestion, no matter where found, whether in the
city or in the individual himself, is unnatural; and, consequently, in every instance, it breeds disease.

Nature is an equalizer. Nature levels things. In the
country, nature makes men strong in their normal desires,
in their enjoyment of work, and in their fondness of
pleasure. To be sure, there are exceptions in all things.
There may be Christs in the city, just as there may be
degenerates in the country. The degenerate, however,
lives in the country for no great length of time. Degeneracy and aloneness do not go together. Vices segregate.
There is seldom to be found an immoral or degenerate being living alone. The simplicity and the solitude of country life is attractive to the good man, the man full of
manhood and strength. He naturally avoids congested
districts and congested conditions. He recognizes the need
of space for breathing and living. In all things, there is

its appropriate compensation. Nature apportions and distributes wisely. The city affords such advantages as wealth and numbers can give. The country affords such benefits as result from simplicity and natural environments.

All things in nature seek their level. The weak, the degenerate, the abnormal, the immoral, cannot live alone. Being unnatural, and having no strength within themselves, nothing to support them, they seek others of like nature. There is a law of gravitation that rules even men. The weak are not content to be by themselves for any great length of time. They must have companionship. Their companionship is ever with those of like nature. They must lean upon others; and they choose those upon whom to lean who are similar in thought and nature to themselves. With the healthy and strong man it is different. There is within him a strength, a manhood, that is sufficient in itself to keep him contented. And, even when he feels the necessity of support, he leans upon nature, and upon nature's provisions, and there finds joy, peace, contentment, and happiness. Further proof of the fact that all things seek their level is seen in the inclination of those who are past their prime to seek city life. The man who is no longer in full strength, no longer able to follow the vocations that belong to the farm and its pastoral life, begins to long for the city or the town. If possible, he frees himself from the responsibilities of the farm. This is not because city or town is more natural or more favorable, but because manhood is waning. He is no longer able to lean upon his own manliness and strength. He seeks conditions that afford close contact with others. Those upon whom he leans in the new environment may likewise be waning in manhood and strength. This is only a natural manifestation of the law of attraction. He is content to find support among those of like status with himself.

Throughout the Hebrew Scriptures, we find inculcated the great law of naturalness and manhood and strength. Not much is said concerning immorality or concerning the future life except the simple statement that he was "gathered unto his fathers" or that God had "called him unto Himself." Why is this? Why does the book that contains the foundation of all physical, moral, and divine laws have so little to say in regard to the future state of the soul? Is it not because the law of naturalness and manliness, the law of health and strength, includes all other laws? Is it not because, through the observance of this law, the matter of morals and of a future existence takes care of itself? The great masters of old, the ancient prophets, the wise sages, recognized the fact that, if a man follows a natural occupation, under natural, creative conditions, living much in the open air, following pastoral pursuits, health and strength are to be expected. To be strong and healthy is an assurance of a strong and healthy mind. A strong and healthy mind is the moral mind. Immorality never dwells long with strength and manhood. From every point of view, manhood is the opposite of weakness, immorality, and depravity. Moreover, the prophets and lawgivers of old recognized that, where there is manliness and manhood in all its glory, one is sure to live a life that is full of peace and glory and free from blemishes. As the future life is a continuation of the present, they recognized that the one who had lived such a life, on passing into another state, was "gathered unto his fathers," or "unto the Father."

In the Hebraic Scriptures, we find many indications of a belief in immortality. In addition to the possession of health and strength, manliness and selfhood, the ideal of immortality is pointed out to man. The prophets are said to have spoken "face to face with God." This indicates a consciousness of Oneness with the Infinite, and brings with it Individuality and Conscious Immortality.

How infinitely superior is the doctrine of ancient prophets and sages, with their ideal of manhood and strength, to the doctrine of later philosophies and religions, which inculcate the belief that physical strength and health are antagonistic to spiritual welfare, that earthly joys are to be refused, that earthly possessions are a snare and a delusion.

A comparison of conditions as they are at present and as they were in former times favors the days of prophet and sage. True it is, to be sure, that among men of old existed weaknesses, diseases, abnormalities, and crimes. But they were the result of depression and congestion; and, when these were removed, illness took its flight. Yet, in those days, there was not the demand for almshouses, insane hospitals, and other centers of refuge for the afflicted. These are products of civilization—a civilization characterized by negative, destructive doctrines of life. Out of those who should have been men and women full of life and vitality, full of joy and happiness, fit subjects for the realm of bliss that has been the dream of the ages, the characteristic doctrines of so-called civilization have made weaklings and vampires upon society.

Without a reasonable degree of health and strength, which is the indication of a natural, normal life, there can be no manhood, no manliness, manifesting in morality. Furthermore, where there is no manhood, there can be no Godhood (Goodhood), no Sonship with the Father, who manifests through all that is natural, all that is glorious, all that is pure and lovable. When an animal is diseased, we call it impure and unfit for man. But, when man is diseased, a distorted and perverted philosophy gives him credit for great purity, being deluded by the belief that he has much of goodness, much of God, within him. How inconsistent is the belief of man! How little logic in his thinking and in his acceptance of facts! His sense of fitness, how beclouded through living under unnatural conditions! When unnatural, abnormal conditions give way, and normal, healthful conditions take their place, great transformations may be expected. Then will health on the three planes of existence—physical, mental, and spiritual—be recognized as an essential to manhood and manliness; and manhood and manliness will be recognized as essentials in him who seeks Godhood.

CHAPTER THIRTEEN

*Neither wisdom nor goodness is indicated by renunciation
of earthly possessions.*

Through a strange misconception of life, it has been
falsely claimed that renunciation of the world, earthly
possessions, and material blessings is a sure indication
of greatness of soul.

If it were a fact that life in and of itself is an evil
or a misfortune, this might be true. But neither reason
nor normal instinct sanctions the doctrine that life is an
evil. Nor is there any ground for the belief that the All
Father sanctions such a doctrine. And, beyond all possibility of contradiction, this doctrine has never been sanctioned by those who travel the path of wisdom. More
than this, the philosophy that throws a false glamor over
renunciation of material interests has its origin in negativeness. It is a destructive doctrine, and needs to be ef-
faced from the minds and the hearts of men. It has already played havoc with many lives, and has thrown vast
numbers into a state of negativeness, from which it is difficult to recover. Those who are too negative to put forth
effort to obtain earthly possessions have eased their own
consciences by claiming that earthly treasures are detrimental to spiritual welfare.

The blessings of earth are not condemned by the
Father of all. Nor are they destructive elements in disguise, come to lead man astray, to lead him away from
the true life, away from the goal of Immortality. On
the contrary, earthly blessings obtained without harm or
loss to others are actually incentives to the better life. They

help to make life worth living. They are incentives to greater effort and to greater achievement. He who obtains earthly pleasures through his own efforts appreciates them and extracts eternal good from them.

It is a provision of the Divine Law that man gains beauty and strength through effort. Effort is the gateway to the highest life possible for man to know. The ideal of effort calls for a type of self-denial that is overlooked as such by those who advocate negative doctrines. It demands that man shall deny himself the privilege of an inactive, negative life. To some, it would be a great hardship to be compelled to put forth effort. To some, it is a great privilege, an indescribable pleasure, to be permitted to indulge in lethargy and inactivity. Their natures are so negative that lethargy and inactivity are the only enjoyments. Ease and inertness are the natural states of negative natures. Such is not the case with normal active beings. The normal being takes delight in activity and growth and changes. The doctrine of self-help, of effort, of work, of development, leads a man to fulfil the destiny of his creation. Any other type of life leads away from the ideal of beauty and strength of character.

In order that life may be sustained on the earth, it is necessary that some shall make an effort to produce those things which are necessary to life. It is possible for each man to produce three or more times as much as he requires for his own consumption. But there are many—the aged, women and children—who are not producers or creators. These must be provided for. Each normal man should, therefore, be a creator of from three to five times the material he requires for himself alone. Moreover, when we consider the vast number of drones, actual vampires, who live, but who labor not, we find that another ratio of one or two must be added to the sum total for whom the real man must create or produce. That this is so is due to abnormal economic and industrial conditions. But, in far too many instances, the non-producers are the very ones who teach negative, destructive doctrines—the evil of earthly possessions and the renunciation of earthly pleasure and earthly gain. This they do either because they are ignorant of all fundamental laws of life or because they desire to blindfold the eyes and to blunt the understanding of those who labor and produce, of those who feed them. Through this type of teaching, producers are lec to class the useless, negative, do-nothing, possess-nothing life as divine and blessed of God, and to consider themselves as honored among men in that they are able to support this class of teachers.

But the awakening is coming. Men are beginning to understand that the first great command of the All Father, "By the sweat of thy brow shalt thou live," includes not only the teeming millions who do labor, but also the multitudes of men who have for centuries lived without useful toil, without effort, simply because they have been enabled to enslave thousands through their destructive doctrines.

Renunciation of the blessings of life, of joy, and of happiness is no indication whatever of godliness. On the contrary, when our eyes are fully opened to the divine truths, we are convinced that it is a mark of degeneracy. It is a process of eternal night, which has begun in the lives of men who are still on the earth. The process of eternal day, on the other hand, is already begun for those who are putting forth conscious effort to reach Godhood through manhood. For those who are living in the daylight, the method and the ideal is neither denial nor renunciation, but self-assertiveness and self-exertion.

Many blessings, this earth of ours can give. Good and pleasant are the delicacies that nature provides for food and drink. Nor are they denied man to enjoy. Sweet

is the rest that comes after the toil of a useful life. Sweet
is the love that is ours honestly won from our fellow trav-
ellers. In many other forms and in countless ways come
the blessings of earth to man. These are not curses in
disguise. They are actual blessings. We have earned them
through effort. That which man earns is not a curse. Nor
is it productive of harm. That which has been honestly
and legitimately earned helps to build up, to make one
stronger, to give one wisdom. Through wisdom, he gains
those things which are truly worth while. Not through
renunciation of earthly possessions does man obtain peace
and joy, happiness and contentment. Nor indeed can it
be said that he obtains peace and joy, happiness and contentment necessarily and invariably, through, or by means
of earthly possessions. Neither renunciation nor possession can, of itself, be considered a sure sign of peace and
happiness. Nevertheless, it must be admitted that earthly
possessions are by no means antagonistic to a pure and
guileless spirit. The conditions of living on the earth demand that man shall provide, for himself and those dependent upon him, not only food, shelter, raiment, and other
necessities of life, but also a reasonable degree of education, culture, and social enjoyment. These things the normal man craves. And rightly so. There is joy and zest
in putting forth effort to obtain these. The effort and
the ability necessary to secure these is one feature of peace
and happiness. Through well-earned effort, through the
ability to secure the necessities and the cultural advantages
of life, and through proper use of them, does man obtain
peace and joy, happiness and contentment. The consciousness of honest and legitimate effort gives ownership both
its right and its pleasure. He who, through honest toil
and exertion, has earned the right to possession knows
the joy and the pleasure of possession.

Not so with him who has renounced earthly blessings,

with him who regards life itself as evil. To him in his
dormant state, not truly earning and deserving the temporal blessings of life, they grant little comfort and cheer.
Apparently, he needs little in order to live. Nevertheless,
during the term of life all told, he requires a great deal.
Not having earned this, but having obtained it through the
efforts of others, he is doubly a vampire on society—first,
in that he lives on what does not properly belong to him,
second, in that he has taken from others what does rightly
belong to them. He may indeed train himself into a self-
deluded satisfaction, regarding his life as righteous and
godly; nevertheless, his conscience is so benumbed by the
hypnotic effect of his erroneous philosophy that it grants
no comfort or cheer. There is a vast difference between
a conscience that fails, through inertness, to prick, and a
conscience that affords positive comfort through a sense
of having done one's best. Were his teachings a positive
good to mankind, it might readily be conceded that they
should earn for him a livelihood. But, considering that
they are a positive harm, in that they advocate a life of
inertness and inactivity, it can scarcely be claimed that
through his doctrines he deserves the recompense of daily
need.

Renunciation belongs to the undeveloped, possibly to
the aged man who has used up all his energies, all his
virility, all his vitality, and has reached that stage of life
in which effort is no longer desirable or natural. To these,
it may be conceded that renunciation is right. But to the
man of good body and good mind, it is a sin—a sin, in
that it is a violation of the law of one's own being, a sin
that eats out the very life of the soul and brings the
individuality to a state of senility or impotence, and ends
in the night of desolation.

The healthy-minded are willing to put forth effort,
every effort in their power. Every new effort brings still

greater strength and power to be used in still more profitable and more availing effort. The healthy-minded seek
work that is a test of strength in order to gain strength
and self-reliance. The unhealthy mind is responsible for
the doctrine of renunciation. Such a mind, weakened and
imbecile, cannot understand the law of "the survival of
the fittest." Therefore, not willing to meet the conditions
of the law by putting forth effort, they formulate a doctrine based on weakness. By dressing it in the garb of
divinity, they prey upon those who produce by putting
forth effort.

In ages past, it was considered that the weak-minded
and the insane were especially blessed of the gods. They
were set apart as favored ones, and they received the most
deferential treatment. Nor was anything denied these unfortunate ones. A similar idea obtains today in regard to
those who live an effortless, useless life, asking alms in
order that they may live. Even men otherwise strong and
powerful, and having creative and productive ability, set
apart, as favored of the gods, those who teach a doctrine
of renunciation and inactivity. In the last analysis, it is
the same error of thought that tenders respect for the
one class and for the other.

Men have not fully awakened to the fact that,
unless prevented by reasons that are beyond control, only
those who labor are deserving. It must be remembered,
however, that mental power and skill expended in productive channels are to be classed among the labor that is
deserving. Labor, toil, effort, self-exertion, self-assertiveness, by no means need indicate slavish drudgery and uninviting conditions. The life of effort that is most deserving often manifests in an expenditure of mental power
and soul force and nerve vitality little dreamed of by the
manual laborer. Yet such a life may be a fitting illustration of the effort that deserves. Also to the unskilled

laborer, such a life may seem to be an idle life, simply because he has no conception of the expenditure of vitality necessary to mental work.

This same negative philosophy, which has been the cause of making imbeciles out of those who should have been engaged in useful toil and productiveness, is to be held accountable for child labor and woman labor.

There is nothing to indicate that the Divine Law sanctions compulsory labor of childhood and womanhood. Whether the compulsion is brought about through economic conditions in general or through the greed of grasping individuals, it is not sanctioned by the Divine Law. It is a violation of child nature, a violation of the laws of growth, naturalness, and spontaneity to place the child under conditions that compel it to do one thing, or to toil incessantly, from morning till night. This very thing is required of the child in order that its labor may be productive and profitable to the employer.

Certain conditions belong by divine right to childhood. If these conditions are violated, the child reaps the inevitable consequence of their violation. Four characteristics are pronounced in childhood—the instinct to play, the instinct to learn or to satisfy a normal curiosity, the instinct "to help," and the instinct that demands change and versatility. These characteristics appear at a very early age. They are the divine heritage of the normal child. In them selves, they are good, aye, even *very good*. Through encouragement and proper guiding, they lead the child to manhood and strength. If, on the other hand, these instincts are violated or crushed, a dwarfed, imbecile condition results; and not only is childhood made unhappy and unnatural, but strong, well-developed manhood is impossible.

These normal instincts in the child are easily gratified. The play spirit is a wholesome instinct, which serves to develop the physical and also gratifies the desire to learn. The play spirit may be turned to good account in teaching the child useful tasks and in satisfying the desire to help. Under wholesome, sweet-spirited guidance, performance of simple tasks adapted to his ability affords as much pleasure as unmolested play. It is only normal and natural that the child should learn in very early years the art of usefulness. In early life, while the instinct to help, to learn, to do, to keep busy and active, is pronounced, is the time to form habits—habits in doing the ordinary tasks of the well-ordered home, habits in regard to personal appearance and personal needs. When curiosity is alert in the discovery of the mechanism and the use of the ordinary conveniences of life is the time to teach the child the correct ways and means of applying them to life's comfort.

Under normal home conditions, the instincts of childhood are encouraged and satisfied and turned to good account. Under conditions of child labor, they are crushed and violated. Spontaneity, originality, naturalness, versatility, the play spirit, the disposition to learn—all are crushed and killed under the grind of incessant and monotonous toil of the factory or workshop.

As long as men fail to do their full duty, just that long will child labor (than which what is more contemptible?) continue to exist. Just as long as there are men, multitudes of them, for one reason or another, living upon the labor of others, just that long will it be necessary for children to be taken from their natural state and be forced to do that which should be done by men. Certainly these conditions do not speak well for our religion or for our philosophy. Surely, they are an abomination unto the Lord. Deserving of reproach indeed are those who engage in the unholy traffic of child labor.

The same arguments hold good in regard to woman

labor. There is a sphere of activity that belongs, by nature and by right, to woman. This realm gives her both employment and joy of life. It is a realm of useful service and versatility, affording variety and pleasure. Life in her legitimate realm develops originality, force of character, and graces of heart, and makes her truly a gracious lovable creature. The marts of trade, the fields of production, belong by nature and by right to man. The normal man ought to produce enough for from three to seven persons. If every man did his duty, if every man followed the dictates of true manhood, woman would not need to enter those fields of labor which belong distinctively to man. In her own sphere, she would still have every opportunity for self-development and pleasant employment. She might still realize all those comforts which make life worth the living. When the ideal of manhood holds sway as the standard of life, things will be different; and child labor and woman labor, as known today, will be no more.

The economic conditions that make child labor and woman labor necessary are the direct result of philosophies and doctrines which put a premium on uselessness, on imbecility, on vampirism. They are the direct result of teachings which make men believe that possession and the desire for earthly joy are wrong. They are the natural outgrowth of standards which place a premium on inertness and inactivity.

Let it be noted that the characteristic instincts of the child are, likewise, the characteristic instincts of the normal man and woman. To be sure, they undergo changes and express themselves differently in the mature person; but they are, in reality, the traits that characterize the normal, positive, active personality. As already stated, these instincts are the play spirit, the inclination to learn, the desire to help and to serve, the inclination to keep busy and active, and to enjoy a reasonable degree of change and variety. These are wholesome, normal traits, and, if gratified, will help keep man young, active, alert. Let it also be noted, that these very traits receive the death blow from philosophies that exalt negativeness, inactivity, and renunciation of life's joys. The basis instincts of life are crushed under philosophies based on renunciation. Rather than being a mark of godliness to renounce earthly possessions and earthly joys, it is a mark of impotence and abnormality. That which crushes originality, spontaneity, naturalness, versatility, and fondness of effort and energy crushes manhood and strength. That which crushes manhood crushes and defeats the possibility of Godhood.

No wonder that men who have at heart human good are zealous in their promulgation of a doctrine that exalts manhood and manliness. The need of the hour is teaching that incites men to effort, to action, to the cultivation of strength and power, teaching that incites men to welcome those responsibilities in life which develop strength through the testing of strength. As men accept the doctrine of manhood, as they frown upon those things which cause weakness and inertness in man, and foster slavish and uninviting toil and drudgery on the part of childhood and womanhood, the new age will set in, the enlightened, the godly age. For, then, men will be too manly to do that which is unmanly or to allow it to be done. Consequently, the weak will be forced to become strong or at least to honor the standards of the strong.

This world was not created in order to become a place of sorrow and misery. Nor was it destined as a land in which ignorance and vice should rule. Rather it was created in order to become a heaven of joy and contentment. It is destined as a land in which men might, in the here and the now, taste the joys that come to the enlightened and developed soul. Unless this purpose of creation is being realized, conditions on this plane are unnatural and not sanctioned by the All Creator.

Man came to the earth ignorant and bound by limitations. He came with no experience. He knew not sorrow from joy, nor pain from pleasure. He came that he might free himself from ignorance and limitation. The only way in which it is possible for him to do this is to learn through experience and effort. But, if he accepts the doctrine of renunciation, the undesirability of earthly possessions, the suppression and denial of joy and happiness, how is he to fulfill this purpose for which he was born? To renounce earthly conditions is to refuse to learn lessons and to gain experience therefrom. This in itself is proof of the destructiveness of negative doctrines. They lead men away from the very purpose of creation, and develop in him a spirit of rebellion or antagonism against the very purpose for which he came to earth. Instead of developing the powers inherent in his nature, turning them to good account in benefiting others, and making him master of conditions, negative doctrines dwarf and stunt his abilities and leave him a weak, undeveloped creature, slave to the conditions of life.

To be sure, the experience that develops strength demands contact with sorrow and pain and undesirable conditions. But, when the purpose of life is clearly understood and cheerfully accepted, the blessings of life are far in excess of the sorrows. True it is that between the pleasures and the joys there are long stages of effort, long intervals of labor. But, to the normal mind, there is in labor neither sorrow nor suffering. To the healthful disposition, labor is a delight. Through our efforts, a new creation is opened up to view. The fact of creating and producing is in itself a joy. There is no higher happiness known to man than the consciousness of being a creator and a producer. All too true, sorrows come. But, to the true man, sorrow is like the night. It enables him to distinguish night from day. Night is the time of rest and absorption of strength, so that we shall be prepared for another day of greater effort, so that we shall have the capacity for greater enjoyment and happiness.

Freedom from evil does not result from renunciation. Renunciation and suppression bring no type of freedom. Freedom comes through exchanging ignorance for wisdom, weakness for strength. Denial brings not strength and freedom. Through effort and through persistent use of the power entrusted to us, we gain freedom. Sins of the flesh are no greater than sins of the mind. The thought that is destructive to the self and to others is detrimental, and, therefore, a sin as truly as is the deed indicated by the thought. Desires of the flesh which bring harm neither to the self nor to others are not sinful. They are sinful only when they result in weakness or bondage or destructiveness. Destructiveness in every shade and degree is evil and a grievous error. Then let no one think it godly to renounce and to suppress life's earthly tokens, to deny and to become negative. Renunciation of joys is far from being a mark of godliness.

CHAPTER FOURTEEN

The Kingdom of Heaven is a kingdom of joy and satisfaction.

There is a doctrine claiming that the love of joy is an evil which belongs to the carnal nature, and that, if we do not get rid of this desire for joy, we shall forfeit all possibility of happiness beyond the grave. This, we have been taught, time and again, in philosophy and in religion. There are other negative, destructive doctrines which are part and parcel of this, such as, that natural instincts are destructive to the soul, that life is undesirable and even evil, that to seek happiness in this life is to be denied happiness in the next, and that only the denial of pleasure, happiness, and joy, and the killing out of all that is natural and normal in our natures will lead to happiness in the future life.

One of the greatest truths ever expressed by a world saviour is this:

"Unless ye become as little children, ye can in no wise enter the kingdom of heaven."

Those who most frequently quote this saying emphasize the innocence and guilelessness of childhood. They overlook one of the most pronounced characteristics of the child—its joyousness and delight in living. To the child, living is a pure delight, a delight that is taken for granted. To the child, it as accepted as self-evident that to live and to enjoy is right. This natural child trait—the pure joy of living, the pure delight of existence, the joy that asks no questions, but takes all for granted—the great teacher of men made use of as the foundation of his philosophy of life.

No, a thousand times No, the desire to enjoy and the delight of living are by no means evil. It is not evil for us so to live as to find all the joy possible in life. Our one concern must be that joy is not gained at the expense of another or of our own well-being. Other than this, there need be no anxiety in regard to seeking joy and happiness. There is the possibility of joy at the expense of one's own higher interests. A joy may be temporary and fleeting, leaving in its wake nothing but bitterness and anguish. This is not a true and normal joy. A joy may be for a moment, resulting in hours of anguish. Neither can this be classed as a true and normal joy. This is not the joy for us to seek. The joy to seek is that which brings sorrow and suffering to no one, joy that has no harmful reaction. When we seek and obtain this type of joy, we are innocently joyous like the little child.

Joy is a state of the inner being that indicates growth and development. To him who believes that our natural instincts are destructive, there is no real joy. Neither is there for him true, normal growth and development. Under the false impression that joy is a delusion and a snare, capable of destroying the soul, the very fountain of joy in one's nature is either closed or so embittered that no true joy is to be found. The faculties are benumbed and dwarfed. Normal development, expansion, and unfoldment of character is impossible. The experienced gardener realizes that the roots of the plant must be free from obstructions. The soil must be kept free from stones and other obstacles. Joy is the state of the soul that frees the life of obstructions to growth. Joy keeps the soil mellow so that light, warmth, moisture, and sunshine may easily penetrate to the very roots of existence and liberate nature's pent-up forces.

All erroneous philosophy or religion is deadening to every faculty of the soul. If one really believes that the

natural instincts are evil, he will shun conditions which
are natural. In consequence, through the crushing of that
which is natural, he is made unnatural. Pain and sorrow are the inevitable fruits of such a life. Joy is not
a part of it. He who believes that nature is deceiving,
and that to follow nature is an evil, and is entirely carnal, will also look upon life as an evil. He who does
not believe in the desirability of life certainly is incapable of joy. To the natural human being, the mere fact
of living is a pure joy. An erroneous idea or belief is
"the leaven that leavens the whole lump." It leaves its
poisonous effects in every part of the organism. No ele-
ment of the being escapes its destructive influence.

On the other hand, a wholesome philosophy or religion enlivens and cheers and stimulates to growth every
faculty of the being. The realization that life is joy comes
to those who are natural, to those who are free, to those
who are slaves neither to another nor to an unnatural
condition within themselves. The unnatural condition
may be due to an error of belief or an error of habit or
to an error of disease or poor health. Those who are
racked with disease and pain cannot possibly know the
highest degree of satisfying joy. A diseased and painful
condition is often due to error and falsity of belief. He
who believes in the evil of natural instincts regards nature as evil. Consequently, he will not follow nature's
laws in regard to health. Good health belongs to him who
lives a natural, normal life, in keeping with a natural, normal philosophy of life. Without a normal view of life,
the mind cannot be normal. If the mind and its reflections and views are abnormal, it is impossible for the body
to be in perfect health. Joy in life therefore depends on
naturalness of being and living. Sorrow, pain, and disappointment are the portion of him who is unnatural in
thought and life.

Joy must be interwoven with all things, if life is to be natural and normal. To the true man, all things bring joy. To the man whose mind is free from remorse, each incident and circumstance brings its peculiar shade and degree of joy. There is joy in labor. No matter what it may be, it affords a certain type of joy. To him, the hour of recreation and the hour of rest are a pure delight. There is nothing to distract the mind, nothing to tincture his thoughts with the caprice and the waywardness of life. All things are because they should be. Though there are for him times of sorrow, as must be for all men, his natural and wholesome mind does not interpret them as due to his own shortcomings. He does not brood over them. Nor does he poison his life with bitterness and morbidness. Though there is sorrow, peace is never disthroned.

Peace of mind is the constant possession of the normal mind. This is the characteristic of the natural life. He who lives in harmony with nature and her laws retains peace of mind even amid most strenuous crises. Losing a loved one, he is in deep sorrow. But sorrow does not destroy the peace that passeth all understanding. There may be sorrow and loneliness, but peace of mind withstands every shock and pain. Peace of mind is disthroned only through evil thoughts and acts, and through morbid and destructive beliefs. When peace takes flight, man is in sorrow indeed. Grief and wretchedness are his lot and portion.

To seek joy is as natural as to seek happiness. Both may be found by him who is willing to accept a natural, normal, divine philosophy and to live a natural, normal, godly life. It is left with each individual to make the choice. Each is the judge for himself. Free-will is given to each. He must choose, and as he chooses, so shall it be unto him. He may choose freedom and realize joy

a؟ a natural consequence. He may choose bondage to
some form of unnaturalness and reap the inevitable consequence thereof.

The unnaturalness to which one may be in bondage
presents many forms. It may be disease, morbid and
inert states of mind, the many shades and tints of weakness and cowardice by which one may be enslaved. He
who is so enslaved cannot know true peace and joy. Always present is the phantom of that which binds him, calling attention to his own weakness. He who is in bondage
to anything is in that particular respect bereft of the
childlike spirit. The child refuses to be bound. The child
spurns the idea that joy is evil.

When natural desires are suppressed, the possibility
of joy is reduced or made impossible. In proportion as
the possibility of joy passes, in that proportion do abnormal instincts and desires take the place of joy. These
abnormal instincts and desires, in time, become so established as to seem both desirable and natural, causing those
who are slaves to them to believe that they are preparing
the way for a life of pleasure and happiness in a future
state.

Self-renunciation is opposed to joy. It is the very
opposite of joy. Nevertheless, it has been believed by
many and freely taught that renunciation is the gateway
to a heaven of bliss. But that this is a destructive doctrine is apparent to all who will think. A little attention
to nature's methods and ways reveals the absurdity of
such a doctrine. A study of the great Masters and world
Saviors reveals that not one of them has advocated such
a belief. In nature, the only renunciation is of that which
is useless or destructive. Nature does not renounce activity. Nor does she renounce strength and satisfaction
and happiness. On the contrary, everywhere in nature,
thrift and accomplishment, health and strength, are en-

couraged. It is only through constant creation that nature is enabled to meet the demands made upon her. She is constantly taxed to the utmost to produce enough to satisfy the needs of those dependent upon her. Consequently, she is actively creating and producing. In nature, this iron law is constantly in operation: that which does not produce, that which does not yield profit, must give place to that which is productive and profitable. Through this law, nature is constantly preaching against renunciation.

Akin to the sense of enjoyment is that other passion known as affection. Affection for anything or anyone, no matter what the degree of affection, brings joy. And the more highly evolved the human being becomes, the deeper and the more sincere will become the affection of such an one for those who are near and dear. Nor does affection stop with mere pleasure and satisfaction. It produces comeliness and strength of soul. The soul's affection will come, in time, to be all-inclusive in its scope and its embrace. The cloak of charity and freedom, it spreads over all; although personal affection and admiration, it cannot bestow upon those who wilfully bind themselves to falsity of belief and to error of ways. There is sympathy and charity for all, even the wayward and the ignorant and the cruel, and those who know not the Divine Law. Charity grants to each man his freedom and right of choice, but, by no means, does charity sanction and endorse the choice of slavery to ignorance, error, and negativeness.

The doctrine of renunciation maintains that affection binds man to his kind and to things of the earth; whereas, his affection should bind him only to the things of heaven. Nevertheless, no one can deny that we are taught in Holy Writ to love one another and to be "kindly affectionate." Love is affection in the highest degree. Love begins on the earth. Love for God begins on the earth plane and must be cultivated on the earth plane. Love for God is grown through love for one's fellowmen. He who loves not his fellows and has no affection for his kind, his friends, his near of kin, is incapable of love for God. The heart that is filled with illusions on earth can scarcely become free from them immediately after the earthly casing is thrown off.

The doctrine of non-renunciation of joy maintains that affection for the treasures of heaven is developed through, and by means of, affection in earthly relationships. Rather than renouncing affection, one should cultivate it. Love for friend and family and neighbor is the kindergarten of love for God. The ideal of health and strength, of grace and beauty of character, is to be encouraged, as means of developing comeliness of soul. The natural ties of home and community are harbingers of good. Through devotion and loyalty in human relationships, through service and helpfulness in every department of human interests, the soul becomes strong and powerful and comely, qualified to meet the demands of a higher plane. Therefore, man should diligently seek those relationships on earth which fit him to enjoy the realities of existence on any plane. Joy comes through the power to serve, the power to help, those whom we love. Thus, health is a condition of joy because it enables us to do and to serve. For the same reason, strength is a condition of joy. Without health and strength, the highest degree of joy is impossible. According to the doctrine of joy and happiness, all those states and conditions in life which are denounced and discouraged by negative doctrines are to be cultivated and encouraged.

He who is unable to know joy and happiness on the earthly plane is not far advanced in the scale of spirituality. He who knows not joy and happiness knows not God.

Joy, happiness, health, strength, are a part of the divine nature. They are essentials of creative ability; and God is, essentially, now and always, a Creator. Weakness and illness, misery and wretchedness, impatience and inertness —these things are, now and always, destructive, and are to be classed among the things that pass away. They interfere with creative ability and hold man on the plane of non-productiveness. They are the conditions that must give place to elements of power and productive skill. They are evil because they are non-producing, because they are non-fruitful. He who follows the law of renunciation follows the negative law of non-productivity. Joy and happiness are elements of spirituality. They are incentives to usefulness and kindness to others, incentives to service and devotion and loyalty. They are natural traits of the productive, fruitful life.

"Seek ye first the kingdom of heaven and all these things will be added unto you."

Seeking the kingdom of heaven certainly is not to seek sorrow, indifference, imbecility, and inertness. One does not need *to seek,* in order to find these things. One needs only to renounce active, positive virtues and, to do nothing at all except idle away strength in order to obtain sorrow, indifference, imbecility, and inertness. But, in order to have health and strength, in order to gain possession of those things which bring joy and happiness, peace and contentment, man must *seek.* He must put forth effort. He must free the mind of undesirable habits. He must fight and struggle for the sake of gaining strength. He must do his duty to his fellow man. This ideal and standard of life calls for activity, industry, usefulness, service. It calls for the joy of effort. This is seeking the kingdom of heaven. Mere introspection, meditation, reflection, and the contemplation of lofty truths is not enough. Seeking the kingdom of heaven demands an active, positive life of usefulness among men.

Joy in the heart is an indication of having found the kingdom of heaven. He who has joy in his heart is to that extent in the kingdom. The joy that results from doing right is the joy of the kingdom. To continue in the way of life that brings joy, is to continue in the kingdom. The kingdom of heaven is nothing more or less than the kingdom of satisfaction, or the plane of satisfaction. When there is peace and satisfaction of mind and soul, then man is truly entered into the kingdom of heaven. It is a kingdom of joy and gladness.

Blind faith cannot free one from sorrow. We may have all possible faith in a negative doctrine, and yet be full of suffering and sorrow. Where suffering and sorrow abound is not the state of bliss and satisfaction. Faith without works, faith without demonstration, is dead. If we have faith and if we work and thereby obtain, then is our faith of the kind that results in salvation. Salvation is freedom from things that are undesirable. If we have faith in God, faith that He will give us happiness, but have not that faith which causes us to meet the conditions of happiness, then we shall reap disappointment. In like manner, if we have faith that God will give us health, but have not the faith that causes us to obey the laws of health, we shall reap disappointment. Our faith is blind and dead, and brings forth no fruits. We may have faith that we shall be happy in a future state; but, unless we actively put forth effort to obtain happiness and to give happiness to others in this life, here and now, we are not qualified for happiness in any state.

Since joy is the result of doing well, since salvation is the result of an active, positive faith manifesting in works, there is no ground for the doctrine of renunciation and inactivity. Think not that, after a life of renunciation, joy and happiness will come to you when the body is cast aside. For, if you do not so live as to find peace and joy here and now, how is it possible to know them on any other plane or in any other sphere?

Learn from the child, which finds joy and happiness in every breath it takes, joy in play, joy in food and drink, joy in work, joy in all things that belong to life.

"Unless ye become as little children, ye can in no wise enter the kingdom of heaven."

Accept the philosophy of joy.   Accept a natural, though divine, philosophy of life. Live the philosophy of joy. Live a natural, divine philosophy of life. And the kingdom of joy, the kingdom of heaven, shall be yours.

CHAPTER FIFTEEN

Suffer not injustice to be done.

For the past few centuries, a double standard a double law, totally contradictory, has been taught mankind—that is, the doctrine of non-resistance and the doctrine of punishment for wrong-doing. As generally understood, these standards are in conflict one with the other. For this reason, justice has fled; and it is a matter of influence as to who is punished and who is not punished.

The principle of non-resistance, rightly understood, is a very important aspect of the Divine Law. But, through prevalent misconceptions and misrepresentations, it has been carried to absurd extremes, and has been woefully perverted. Instead of making men out of criminals, it has often resulted in making criminals out of men. Instead of making men strong and self-reliant, it has made them weak and omnipotent. Rightly understood, the law of non-resistance is positive, demanding positive strength on the part of him who obeys it. As generally accepted, it is a negative standard, tending toward lethargy and inertness on the part of him who follows it.

The laws of resistance, non-resistance, and of punishment are one and the same. These three are indeed one, viewed from different angles. The laws of justice demands a supplement. The necessary supplement and corollary of justice is mercy. The mistake of those who carry the law of non-resistance to extreme limits is in thinking that there is a conflict between mercy and justice. The two are in perfect harmony. Resistance, non-resistance, justice, and mercy are in exact accord one with another.

A prevalent misconception of the law of non-resistance goes to the extreme of resisting nothing—not even wrong and injustice. This extreme interpretation of non-resistance leads to the attitude of utter indifference—the very worst feature of negativism. It accepts, absolutely and with no qualification, the principle, "Whatever is, is best." In regard to the errors and shortcomings and weaknesses of one's own nature, it puts forth no effort toward improvement. Its indifference toward error and injustice may become so pronounced as to amount to the same thing as sanction of error and injustice. This conception of non-resistance strikes at the very roots of growth and development. It leads to inertness of the most formidable type. It sanctions and encourages a tolerance that is beyond reason and good judgment. It is directly opposed to development of manhood and manly powers and virtues. Thus, it leads away from the possibility of Godhood.

This misconception is so subtle and delusive that it is making rapid inroads upon the minds and the hearts of the people. It is an easy road to travel, calling for no effort whatever—easy because it is a downhill path. It is attended, nevertheless, by dangers unforeseen and unsuspected. And, ere he is aware, the one who travels this path is plunged into perilous situations, from which he is scarcely able to extricate himself.

Since this misconception in regard to the law of non-resistance is so delusive and leads to such errors, is it any wonder that the alarm is being sounded? Is it any wonder that those who comprehend the disastrous results of this misconception are doing all in their power to avert the ill effects of this promulgation? Let nothing be done or said to cast a reflection upon the reality or the importance of the law of non-resistance. There is such a law. More than this, it is one of the most important expres-

sions of the Divine Law. The effort that is being made is
to avert the errors growing out of an extreme misconception in regard to the meaning of the law.

The harmony that exists between the laws of resistance, non-resistance, and justice can best be made clear
through the use of illustrations.

Suppose, walking down the street, you see a human
brute abusing a child or a defenseless woman. Holding
to the extreme view of non-resistance, your reflections are
somewhat after this fashion: 'None of my business, this.
Each individual is free to do as he pleases. What is it
to me? Am I my brother's keeper? Am I judge as to
who deserves abuse? What law gives me right to deal
out justice or punishment to the guilty?'

With these reflections you pass by. But how can
there be manhood in this disposition of the difficulty?
How can there be a conscience pure and undefiled? By
allowing the abuse of helpless ones to continue, you become party to the abuse. By offering no resistance, you
sanction injustice and cruelty. Is this the part of a true
man? Is this the part of courage and true manliness,
"to pass by on the other side," leaving innocence and help-
lessness to suffer ill treatment at the hands of the cruel
or the irresponsible? No, a conscience that satisfies itself with the motive of non-resistance under such conditions is a conscience that has withered and dwindled away
from non-use. Through inertness and stagnation, it has
lost its power to prick and sting. It has made a god of
indifference and non-interference with others. In many
instances, non-interference is a virtue to be highly commended. But, in the case of cruelty to the helpless when
it lies within one's power to prevent, it is far from being
commendable. He is worthy indeed of bearing the form
and the figure of a man, who dares to rebuke criminal
acts and to succor the defenseless and the needy. We

may be ourselves powerless for rendering help; but, in that case, we can at least call the attention of one who is in a position to exercise control over abuses.

The law of non-resistance is perverted in the conclusion that we are not our brother's keeper. To exercise no concern in regard to the welfare of another, even though he be an enemy or a stranger, is carrying the principle of non-resistance to unreasonable extremes. The strong man finds satisfaction in the thought that he is qualified to be, in measure, his brother's keeper. He counts it an honor to his manhood to be entrusted with the right and the privilege of helping and serving others. His sense of justice and right cannot bear the shock of seeing the helpless abused or ill treated without offering protest. To pass injustice by without protest belongs to the errors and misconceptions connected with the law of non-resistance, not to the law itself. The law of non-resistance honors the standard that, under reasonable limits, we are our brother's keeper.

The law of injustice includes man's relation to the animal kingdom as well as the human. As in the case of his neighbor, man's attitude toward the animal kingdom depends upon his disposition of the law of non-resistance. With many, there seems to be a conflict between the law of justice and the law of non-resistence. The law of justice demands protection of the helpless. The extreme view of non-resistance sanctions indifference and non-interference with the actions of others. Abuse and injustice toward one of the animal creation calls for rectification. An unreasonable view of non-resistance conflicts with the standard of justice and says, 'No, non-interference is best.' Those who accept the unreasonable view ignore cruelty to animals. Seeing a seeming conflict between the standard of justice and non-resistance, they choose the left-hand path, that of negativeness and indifference.

It is the duty of the strong to protect the weak. Any interpretation that excuses the strong man from this obligation strikes at the very roots of strength and manhood in his nature. To exercise strength, to turn it to good account in the protection of the unfortunate, to demonstrate manliness and courage in favor of the needy—this and this alone gives man the right to strength. Under the iron law of nature, through non-use, power and manhood forfeit their right to existence. The hand that refuses to perform the duties of a useful hand, preferring to hang idle and useless from the shoulder, ceases to be a hand that is capable of usefulness. Likewise, the individual that exalts the standard of non-resistance to the extent of refusing to live a life of usefulness and activity among men, refusing to protect the needy as opportunity affords, loses the power of usefulness and manhood. Through loss of manhood and manly virtues, he forfeits the possibilities of Godhood. And let it be remembered that manhood is the gateway to Godhood.

There is no reason for our being unduly zealous in observing occasions of cruelty toward others. It is not for us to go out of our way in search of injustice and mal-treatment. Guardianship over others is not a thing to be coveted for its own sake nor for selfish purposes. Generally speaking, punishment of injustice does not belong to man. Not punishment of the guilty, but protection of the innocent, is the point under consideration. The principle that deserves emphasis is that man shall not shrink from his duty nor shirk responsibility when duty and responsibility are plain. To do so means weakness. It does not pay to hide behind the cloak of deference to the law of non-resistance.

Thus far, our illustrations have had to do with the principle of non-resistence in connection with other than ourselves. What about the law of non-resistance in its bearing upon ourselves? Are there erroneous, unreasonable views of the law in its application to the individual himself?

To be sure, there are grievous misconceptions of the law in its bearing upon individual growth and development. It has already been pointed out that failure to meet the conditions of manhood and strength when the law of justice calls for active succor or protection of others results in weakness to him who so fails to do his duty. It remains to be emphasized that weakness is the reward of him who exalts the law of non-resistance to unreasonable limits in regard to his own personal growth and development.

By many, by those who exaggerate the law to extreme proportions, the attitude of non-interference is taken toward one's own weaknesses and shortcomings. A reasonable degree of patience is commendable. But patience that reaches the limit of ignoring defects when effort would have removed them has passed beyond the boundaries of a virtue. In the case of many who are eager in the cause of soul development, the methods of development are so negative as to border close to non-resistance itself. Even prayer may become so passive as to be ineffectual. Something more positive than "Nevertheless, not my will but thine be done" is demanded in gaining the victory over uprisings of the carnal nature. In human nature generally, strenuous and persistent effort and positive watchfulness are demanded, to withstand the possibility of being overtaken by a sudden outburst of anger or jealousy or some other manifestation of carnality. He who lapses into the state of indifference or non-interference has already lost ground in regard to self-mastery.

The ambitious soul aims at mastership, mastery over himself. Mastership demands zealous care, constant watchfulness, a powerful will, and an active, positive attitude of mind. Remarkable power of resistance is his who has attained self-mastery to any appreciable degree.

There are other aspects of the law, however, in its application to ourselves. If a thief enters our house with intent to steal that which is ours by right of honest effort; if wayfarers trespass on our grounds, trampling under foot grass and flowers, destroying fruits for which we have labored; if neighbor's cattle break their bounds and devastate our fields, damaging our sun-kissed crops; if a servant in the home proves faithless and pilfers both coin and produce—under such conditions as these, as well as many others that may arise, is there nothing to be done by way of self-protection? Under such circumstances, does the law of non-resistance conflict with the standard of justice toward ourselves?

No, non-resistance is not to be identified with non-interference under such circumstances as these. Non-interference, under such conditions, brands one either as weak and cowardly or as ignorant of the law. If one hides behind the screen of non-resistance in his disposition of such difficulties, he classes himself among those who honor not the law, but a misrepresentation of the law. He in whom remains one ounce of manhood must realize that non-interference is but to injure those who are injuring us by their trespass and outrage. If it falls within our power to prevent the thief from taking that which is ours, prevention is a kindness to him. To offer no resistance to that which is a positive injury to ourselves, other things being equal, is a positive injury to the one who would cause us injury. To allow another without resistance to take from us that which is ours, is to be party to the thievery. What we owe to another, we owe also to ourselves. If we are responsible for preventing crime against another when within our power, we are also responsible for preventive measures in the case of attempted wrong to ourselves.

Again, what disposition is to be made of the law of non-resistance in the attitude of the parent toward the child? Of the school master toward those under his care? Of the employer toward the workman in his shop? Is the law of non-resistance here to be identified with the principle of non-interference? Is there a conflict between the standard of justice and the principle of non-resistance? The child in its innocence is liable to encounter danger. It is liable to fall into wayward habits, detrimental to itself. At times, it is in need of reproof and correction and careful guarding. Is the parent's authority to be hampered by an erroneous conception of the law of non-resistance? The boy in the school room, possibly the youth within college walls, is forming habits that are decidedly detrimental to his own welfare. Shall the teacher, under a false impression of the virtues of non-interference, leave him unrestrained when possibly a heart-to-heart talk concerning the error of his ways would set him aright? The clerk at the counter, the accountant at the desk, the salesman on the road, may be laboring under tension or under a temptation peculiar to his temperament. Let the employer open his eyes to the personal needs of him who is under his employ. Let him give word of cheer, advice, or rebuke according to need, rather than screen himself behind the weak excuse of non-resistance.

The principle of action is twofold. It affects both the doer and the receiver. If one injures us, by that very act, he also injures himself. For this reason, it is right for us to prevent wrong-doing to ourselves if it lies within our power so to do. So exact is the law of justice, however, that, if another intentionally harms us and we are ignorant of his deed and undeserving of harm, the deed reacts upon the doer harmfully, while we reap benefit therefrom. To permit wrong doing with indifference, is to cause weakness and loss to him who does the wrong.

It makes him weaker rather than stronger. Whoever adds to the weakness of another, to that extent does him an injustice. No matter if one's excuse is righteous non-interference with others, it is an injury to the one whom he might have helped.

The prevalent misconception regarding the law of non-resistance has its origin in a desire for purity of heart and conscience. Under circumstances that prompt resistance or interference, the elements of ill-will and impatience easily creep into the heart; retaliation and revenge often are uppermost in the motive. This fact has led to the feeling that resistance in itself is wrong. The spirit of ill-will and bitterness pricks the conscience and stings the soul. To obviate this difficulty and to secure purity of conscience, has led to the belief that resistance and interference with the actions of others is a sin. Thus, non-resistance, in the sense of indifference and non-interference with the actions of others, has come to be viewed as a virtue. This has been thought to be the only type of non-resistance that gives the consciousness of a pure heart and a clean motive and a clear conscience.

The fact that there is a pricking of conscience indicates that something is wrong. But—and this is the point to be emphasized—not resistance is wrong, nor interference, but the ill-will that accompanies resistance and interference. Not prevention is wrong, but the spirit back of preventive measures. The censure and the condemnation and the impatience and the bitterness that attend prevention—this is wrong. The fact that there is pricking of conscience indicates that something needs to be eliminated. The error has been in thinking it right to eliminate resistance itself, rather than the bitterness and the ill-will that attend resistance.

Non-resistance demands the elimination of bitterness and revenge and hate and every form of ill-will from the

heart of him who resists. The Divine Law sanctions resistance against error and crime. It sanctions prevention of wrong. The Law sanctions effort, will-power, and
self-mastery. Interference with others when circumstances
warrant, it also sanctions. A reasonable degree of control and authority over others when one's relation with
them permits, also receives the sanction of the Divine
Law. But, always and everywhere, the Law demands the
elimination of every type and description of ill-will and bitterness and revenge toward those with whom we deal.
This is the feature of non-resistance that must be emphasized and re-emphasized.

Let us prevent suffering. Let us rectify wrongs, and
obviate error and ignorance and crime. Let us succor the
needy, and protect the helpless, both in the animal kingdom and in the human. Let us administer justice as opportunity affords. Let us put forth every effort to
strengthen the cause of right. Let us live an active, positive, useful life among men. *But let us do all in the
spirit of love.*

The law of non-resistance demands that no thought
of hate, no thought of revenge, shall creep in as the motive of our act, but that only the thought of right and
justice shall be the base of our action. Non-resistance ap-
plies to the spirit of action rather than to action itself.
The regeneration of society demands powerful resistance
against the inroads of error, ignorance, and crime. But
equally true is it that the regeneration of society demands
that the spirit of love shall prompt every resistive measure.

Men of strong intellect and superior ability are de-
voting their lives to the cause of peace and arbitration.
They are actively engaged in educating public sentiment
in favor of peace principles. They scatter literature broad-
cast advocating measures that prevent war and bloodshed,

They plead with congresses in favor of passing bills which support the amicable adjustment of difficulties. In the life of him who is actively, definitely, zealously engaged in promoting peace principles and in preventing war and carnage, where does non-resistance come in? Just here— he does what he does in the spirit of love and kindness. He kicks not against the pricks. He does not force his plans upon others. If his preventive measures are defeated, he harbors no grudge or antagonism against his opponent. In that he labors in patience and is preserved in the spirit of love and charity, he honors the law of non-resistance.

The prevalent misconceptions in regard to the law have brought it into great disrepute among strong, right-minded men. In its false representation, the law encourages cowardliness and weakness. In its negative, destructive aspects, the law cultivates in a man the spirit of indifference toward reform and betterment of society. No wonder that true, noble manhood spurns the doctrine of indifference! Rightly understood, the law of non-resistance must appeal to every true, strong, noble-minded man and woman. It honors manhood and strength. In a two-fold manner, it honors strength and courage—the strength and courage to act, and the strength and courage to maintain sweet-spiritedness in the midst of action. The force that might have been squandered in negative, destructive thoughts of ill-will are to be turned to active use in the cause at hand. Thus, strength and force and courage are both intensified and purified. The fact that non-resistance is identified with indifference and non-interference and non-prevention, has brought the doctrine into disfavor among men and women of noble mind and heart. That non-resistance means the spirit of love as basis of resistance and prevention, will bring the law into favor with noble-hearted men and women.

The law of non-resistance in this sense is in perfect accord with the New Commandment. Passivity and indifference in the midst of error and wrong is not a trait of manhood. Activity and effort toward the betterment of self and others, accompanied by the spirit of love—this is a trait of manhood that leads to Godhood.

The law of non-resistance would eliminate, from all preventive measures, the desire to "get even with" or to "get ahead of another." When the heart is free from resentment or ill-will and one puts forth effort against error, ignorance, and sin, he is not resisting evil in the sense of kicking against it; he is simply preventing evil, and promoting the cause of justice and right. If our attitude toward wrong doing is based on the thought of punishment merely, or of dealing out justice to those whom we consider deserving of the hand of justice, then, our attitude is not sanctioned by the true law of non-resistance. Obedience to the law of non-resistance demands that our desire shall be for justice and righteousness and for the betterment of him whose ways we would rectify. If our mind is tinctured with revenge and resentment and ill-will and the desire to "get even," we are not fit subjects for exemplifying the standard of justice.

What about punishment, by the state, of the so-called criminal?

It would be difficult for any one to prove that the system of punishment as carried out at the present time has the sanction of the Law of God. Who can successfully maintain that it is free from hate and revenge? Seldom is the criminal punished on the merits of his deed alone. More often he is punished because of the hate and suspicion and fear of society generally.

There is a law of punishment—a law that operates through every department of nature. It is not according to man-made code. According to man-made law, the

criminal is punished FOR his sins. According to natural
law, he is punished BY his sins. This principle—that
man is punished *by* his wrong doing, *by* his own ignorance,
error, and sin—must be recognized by the state, before a
just system of dealing with criminals can be established.

Wrong doing is to be ascribed to one or both of two
causes. Either a man does wrong in ignorance of the
laws of life or he does it because he is held by abnormal
tendencies. In either case, the remedy is the same. Little
ground is there for thinking that he is benefitted by con-
finement in a place unfit for human habitation, wherein
body and mind and soul are stunted, wherein every particle of manhood and divinity in his nature is destroyed?
If the cause of his crime is ignorance, he needs instruction and training. If the cause is abnormal tendencies,
he is, likewise, in need of instruction and training. Pris-
ons should be turned into centers, from which men come
forth stronger and better than they went in. Instead of
this, they come out hounded creatures, from which every
shred of manhood has been taken.

Boast as we may of the superiority of the upper classes of society over the lower strata, it remains a fact that,
in every human being, there are traces of superstition, of
ignorance, of ignoble or even criminal tendencies. But
some are more ignorant than others. Some have stronger
tendencies toward wrong doing than others. These are
called criminals. It is only a matter of degree. The
criminal is worse than the more favored.

Life on this earth is our school. If the ignorant and
criminally inclined were given the advantages of an institution that combines in its methods the elements of
workshop and of school, they would imbibe better ideas
of life, as well as learn a useful trade. Men who serve
as teachers in such an institution, coming in close daily

contact with abnormal personalities, would have occasion constantly to apply the principle of non-resistance. Non-resistance, in the sense of indifference, passivity, and non-interference, has no place in the lives of such men. But, of non-resistance in the sense of charity, patience, and sweet-spiritedness, they require a generous fund. Such non-resistance in the midst of activity has its sure reward.

When the correct idea of non-resistance has become established in the hearts of men, a transformation of society will have taken place. Manhood will be the ideal. On right and on left, manhood will be the accepted standard.

"Be a man that thou mayst be a god."

CHAPTER SIXTEEN

The spirit of chivalry and fairydom is constructive in its effects.

Another feature of negativism is to condemn fairy-tale literature and every appeal to the fanciful and the picturesque.

In the age when fairy tales, stories of the spirits of nature, the fairies of flowers and of woodland, were the rule, culture and manhood and chivalry and perfection were at their height. When Greece was at the zenith of its power, when it was a nation of true manhood, when culture had reached its highest estate, at that time, its philosophy was free from elements that are unwholesome and destructive in their effects.

In the present age, alas, only a small percentage of our children are conversant with the fairy tales that gladdened childhood in the ancient days. Instead of the beautiful, soul-inspiring tales of fairydom, we have accounts of unclean spirits and demons—stories which arouse thoughts of suspicion and superstition and fear. This tendency has reached its highest possible point in the stories of malicious animal magnetism of a certain school of philosophy.

It is a noteworthy fact that, in every age of the world, the religion, the philosophy, and the stories for childhood harmonize perfectly. Folk lore and nursery rhymes and ditties all reflect the quality of sentiment entertained by the elders. Tales and fabulous accounts of beast or woodland sprite, formed to please the fancy of childhood, reflect the spirit of the national religion and philosophy.

Greek literature preserves for us a collection of narratives concerning gods and goddesses. A multitude of gods and goddesses, their religion embodied, a superior household of divine beings. Classic myths and legends of the palmy days of Greece serve not only as a means of preserving their philosophy and religion, but as a means of preserving the splendor of their literature for childhood.

The effect that a nation's religion and philosophy has upon its adherents is the ultimate test of its quality and character.

For example, note the Greek religion and philosophy and the effect upon Greek ideals and standards. To all outward appearances, it was a religion and a philosophy of polytheism—in reality, a religion and a philosophy of the utmost deference to the One Supreme God, ruler over all. In their conception of gods and heirarchies, there was nothing more unnatural than there is in the idea of one supreme ruler over a nation or a country, with an extensive retinue of sub-officers and subordinate powers whose function it is to exercise authority and dominion in the department over which they are placed. There is no evidence that the Greeks considered all the gods as THE God. Nor is there any evidence of their believing in polytheism. The individual gods and goddesses were varying expressions or manifestations of the One Great Deity, the One Great Power or Force of Nature. The gods and goddesses were hierarchies over the different departments of nature. They represent different forces; or, to express the thought more accurately, they represent the One Great Force functioning in different ways and in different channels, while the One Supreme Being is the Power or the Being that is, has been, and ever shall be.

In harmony with this doctrine of the Greeks concerning rulership, is the divine ideal placed before man for his attainment—the standard of manhood and individuality and personal responsibility. This ideal of strength and character demanded physical power and endurance. Therefore, perfection of body was the basis on which must be built the superstructure of noble and beautiful character. Consequently, a part of their time and attention was devoted to the requirements of the human form, to exercises, athletic games, swimming, bathing, and other features. Nothing was overlooked in their desire that the body might reach the highest state of perfection. Considering weakness and disease as indications of abnormality, the Greeks put forth unbounded effort to free themselves from weakness and disease of every type and dscription. A beautiful figure, perfect physique, grace of movement and motion, as well as muscular strength and endurance were sought not merely because they are in themselves desirable, but especially because they are the natural basis of noble character.

The Greek ideal of cosmogonic rulership and their ideal of manhood and bodily perfection became chizelled into the form of a national literature, embodying the qualities of elegance, refinement, and strength. For the mature mind, there were philosophic treatises and literary creations, exalting nobility and refinement of character. For childhood, there were myths and legends and fairytales, calculated to guide the child mind step by step to an appreciation of the national religion and philosophy. A nation of athletes, a nation that exalted nobility of character, as well as attractiveness of physique, a nation of culture and refinement—at its height, the Greek nation, in its life and character, reflected credit upon the national religion and philosophy.

Later, in history, we have the tales of chivalry and the ideals of knighthood to satisfy and stimulate the mature mind, and fairies, myths, and legends of a pure type, as incentives to childhood. These reflect a normal and wholesome mind. Only the normal, healthful mind can create and execute literary inventions of this class. Nothing weak and flabby finds place in this type of literature. Heroism, strength, and nobility are everywhere honored. Truth of the highest and purest type is clothed in fanciful designs, and in rich, perhaps even gorgeous, yet picturesque coloring. Knighthood and heroes signify aspects of truth. They represent strong qualities and virtues protecting and guarding the soul in its struggle for supremacy over error and wrong.

Fairies, myths, and legends serve a far more exalted purpose than merely to please the fancy. Like the parable and the allegory, they clothe truth and make abstract ideas tangible. Childhood is the age of imagination. It is the age that pictures and paints in glowing colors and in startling details. Yet, underneath its picturing, is a vein of truth. The fancy of childhood is alive with expectancy and imagination. To the child, flower, tree, animal, stone, is a living creature capable of pleasure and joy, of change and motion. Fairies are the souls of flower, plant, animal, and stone. Water and woodland, grove and meadow, valley and plain, mountain and hillside are peopled with the fairy creations of childhood. When the minds of the elders are filled with tales of gods and goddesses, creatures ideal in their power, strength, nobility and beauty, is there any wonder that literature, art, and song reflect beauty?

When you find a people that believes in the goodness of God, and in the goodness of the ruling powers, in the divine heritage of man, the desirability of life on earth, the possibility of joy and happiness, then, you find a nation that is normal and healthy both physically and mentally. The children of that nation are of healthy minds—minds not filled with tales of evil powers that infest the night time. They are children who do not fear to enter the woodlands alone, as do our children. To the children of today, the woods are filled with evil powers, cruel beings, and demons, hostile to childhood. But to the child in the land where manhood rules, where a constructive religion and philosophy is taught, woodland and field are the playground of angels, gnomes of the earth, guardians of tree and plant and shrub. In all these, the child sees something beautiful, something desirable and uplifting. Though he may scarcely be conscious of it, he sees in the beautiful fairy of the flower the soul of its Maker and the handiwork of the All Creator.

What a contrast between the two ages! What an undesirable heritage is that of the child when destructive negativism holds sway and an unnatural and wholly untrue materialistic teaching has taken everything desirable out of life!

The average child of today does not even enjoy the games that once delighted youth and added health and strength to body and mind. Its tendencies are toward a sedative study, which accomplishes nothing. In far too many cases, the thoughts are poisoned by secret vices which one child teaches the other at school or on the streets, tales of vices which do not even exist and are not possible. Vices that do not exist are twisted in the telling until they form pictures of greater destruction in the child mind. Say what we will, these things are facts. Passing through a crowd of boys and girls ranging from six to twelve, we hear them talking of subjects that would shame their elders because they are unnatural and abnormal.

Yet we boast of the fact that we are living in an age in which children know better than to believe in absurd fairy tales, know better than to believe in Santa Claus, and the Easter rabbit. We boast of the fact that our children no longer believe that a fairy has its home in every flower, that the woods are peopled with nymphs jolly and full of fun. Of these things, we boast, forgetful that the minds of our children are peopled with entities of some sort, if not beautiful creations, kings and queens of fairyland, then demons and monsters of vice and crime. Thoughts are creatures that people the mind. The thought of love and kindness is a beautiful, heaven-born fairy. Thoughts of vice and ugliness are monsters of destruction.

We think only in symbolism. Each thought is a form, each thought is a creative entity. Thought of the tree, of the flower, or the shrub that we admire, is a creature like that of which we think. It is an entity.. Men created the word well when they called thoughts fairies.

As time passed, men became inclined toward a doctrine and a philosophy of weakness instead of one of strength. Naturally, their thoughts turned toward idleness and the desirability of ease and non-effort. They regarded labor as degrading and undesirable, and ease and luxury as the only things worth while. Gradually, in place of tales of beautiful gods and goddesses, in place of dreams of heroes and chivalric knights and winsome maidens, in place of fairydom with its kings and queens of splendor, ever standing ready to grant the fondest wish of the dutiful child, the minds of men become peopled with monsters and demons and devils and every description of taunting creatures destructive and revolting. Since the age of fairy and fable has passed away, literature and art and song reflect morbidness of mind and unhealthful ideals and standards.

With negative, destructive thoughts and the desire to live without honest toil, men began to create and to formulate methods for binding the evil entities that peopled their minds. From that day to this, we have a class of men "who toil not, neither do they spin," but who live on the best of the land, not because they have earned it by honest effort, but because the many are slaves while the few are owners of slaves, because they have been enabled through their negative, destructive philosophy to bind the multitudes. They have taken from men and children the heroic gods, the fairies of the flowers, the nymphs and innocent sprites of water and land. From man, they have taken heroism, individuality, power, glory. Demons, evil influences, evil entities, they have given him. His imagination, they have peopled with evil and destructive horrors, with tortures and distresses. Instead of being surrounded by angelic presences and supernatural powers and forces of goodness and protection, he is haunted by grim messengers of fear and torture, products of a perverted imagination and a troubled conscience. Weakness and disease and a belief in the undesirability of life, they have given him. Through these influences, they are holding the multitudes in slavery—a slavery that is, however, unconscious and willing.

But the new age with its doctrine of manhood has come. Every effort is being made to replace in the minds of men emphasis upon manhood, heroism, and individuality. The desirability of manly courage and positive effort is receiving due emphasis. As love and good-will supplant ill-will and vice, the minds of men will come to be people with beautiful creations. In time, the mind of man will become so pure that soul vision shall be his; and, with purified and clarified vision, he shall see the lovely queen of the flowers, and the spritely nymph of wood and meadow. Again shall the child gain freedom from thoughts of vice and evil; and the morbid will have no attraction for him. Men will understand better how to train the child and how to make conditions suitable for his growth. Where nature and normal conditions govern, evil and destructive tendencies cease to exist.

The New Commandment brings the doctrine of manhood, the desirability of life, the privileges of godhood and joy and happiness, the right of earthly possessions through honest effort. It brings to man the gospel of health and strength. It exalts heroic deeds, the right of the strong to protect the weak, the possibility of being free from hate, from anger, from jealousy and every form of malice. The right to seek love, the right to love and be loved—this the New Commandment teaches. Happiness that is won in this world, joy that is known here and now, is but the beginning, the path, the gate, of the greater joy and happiness in the next world. Unless he finds peace and contentment now and here, he will not be qualified to enjoy it on any other plane. The New Commandment is the gospel of freedom, of strength, of possession. It is the gospel of a healthy body, but it is also the gospel of the Immortal Soul, the privilege of man to become the Son of God. It is the gospel of Sonship with the Father, of Godhood for him who seeks it in the power of manhood.

It is freely admitted that there is what is called the evil or the negative side of nature. It is freely admitted that there are evil entities, and there have always been such entities and influences. They existed even in the golden age of glorious Greece. But it is also claimed beyond the possibility of successful contradiction, that, when man is healthy and normal, strong and godlike, when the mind is free from hate and malice and envy and revenge, these poisonous entities affect him not. They are, to the pure mind and heart, what the poisonous mushroom is to the sun. The sun rises and shines upon the mushroom, and the mushroom shrinks away and is no more. The sun feels not the evil or the poisonous effects thereof. To the sun, it is as though the mushroom had not been. Likewise, to the healthy, normal man, the evil entities and influences that come in contact with him either pass quickly away or they shrink and wither and are no more.

The mind of man is so constituted that it cannot be a vacuum. It must be occupied continually with some thought. Either it is a thought that is constructive and conducive to health and strength and power and creative ability or it is the reverse.

In the universal mind, like the mind of the individual, a certain type of thought holds sway. Its prevailing thought may be along lines of health and strength and man_hood and individuality, including honor, heroism, love, joy, happiness, and righteous possession—the FAIRY type of thought. Or the prevailing thought may be of disease, of weakness, of the undesirability of life, the evil of joy and happiness, the unreality of existence on the earth plane—the DEMON type of thought.

It is for man to choose. As to what his choice has been throughout the ages, literature records. With unerring accuracy, literature and art and song preserves the thoughts that have held sway in the minds of men.

Give us the age of heroic gods, of the One All Powerful, All Creative God over all. Give us the age of chivalry, the age of fairydom. Take away the age of demons and evil entities and malicious thought force.

Give us the age of manhood, the age of strength and achievement. Take from us the age of weakness, and of imbecility. The age of night, take from us, and give us the age of light.

CHAPTER SEVENTEEN

Manhood or degeneracy, which?

In the past gradually, but in the present very rapidly, are men awakening to the fact that creeds and philosophies of the negative type have been the base of life and that they have been leading the race to degeneracy.

These doctrines, which have emphasized the undesirability of life, the sin of earthly loves, and the corrupting influence of material possessions, have spent their force. The world has reached a crisis. It is a question as to what is to be the result. It is to be hoped there will be a turning of the way, a giving up of the old doctrines and philosophies, and the adoption of a code of ethics that teaches manhood—manhood strong and virile, above all else.

It is not intended to convey the idea that negative philosophies have had in view degeneracy of the human race. Far from it. But the fact that their negative principles have influenced the lives of the multitudes, the fact that they have been the base of life and action, makes them responsible for the tendency toward degeneracy.

Conventions are being held from time to time all over the civilized world in the interests of race betterment. But, without exception, the blame is wrongly placed. The remedies suggested are even worse than useless; for they would be destructive to mankind as conditions now are. Eugenics and sexual hygiene are given prominent places in the programs of these conventions.

That eugenics and sexual hygiene are important factors in race betterment is not to be denied. But eugenics grafted to the present creeds and philosophies in their negativeness would bring forth fruit that would utterly dismay those who advocate them. First of all, it is necessary for social and economic conditions to be changed; for eugenics and sexual hygiene can accomplish nothing until the fundamental doctrines of life to which the vast multitudes hold are basically changed. Of what use is race betterment if men believe that life is an evil? Of what use are the teachings of eugenics if men hold to the belief that the body is an enemy to the soul? Without exception, such ideas as these have been taught by the old creeds. And he is looked upon with suspicion who dares to teach true manhood as the base of all things.

When men believe that this life is undesirable and that death is good because it gives entrance to a blessed state in the hereafter, is it to be supposed that they are working for race betterment? Is it to be supposed that they are interested in developing the physical being unto perfection so that it may last beyond the three score years and ten presumably allotted to man? Has not the world been taught, during the past centuries, that the body of man is the repository of evil? Have we not been taught that a strong, vigorous body is the direct enemy to the soul because, in the strong body, there are many passions which lead the soul astray? Not in so many words perhaps, but in principle at least, we have been taught that illness and disease are not something to be shunned and avoided and to be overcome, but, on the contrary, that ill health in no wise interferes with our journey toward bliss. Men have even gone so far as to claim that an illuminated soul may dwell in a diseased, corrupt body. Indeed, what is there in our philosophies to lead to the thought that the state of the body has anything whatever to do with the state of the soul?

Suppose that, for eighteen hundred years, the race had been taught that in order to have a perfect soul it was necessary, first of all, to have a perfect body—a body normal, healthful, and strong—think you that an abnormal outcry in favor of eugenics would now be necessary?

Suppose, during these same centuries, the race had been taught that the All Father sanctions honest labor, that He honors honest accumulation of worldly goods for the sake of the fruits of righteousness thereof, think you that beggarism would be prevalent, on the one hand, and that, on the other hand, those called saints would be eating the fruit of other men's labor? Would this be possible?

If our religion and our philosophies had taught us, during these centuries, that strict obedience to the laws of health is the foundation of spirituality; if they had promulgated the principle that perfection of body is essential to Illumination of Soul, think you that misery and weakness and degeneracy would now be the common lot of man? These conditions would exist only in a limited degree if our philosophies had not been fundamentally wrong, if man had not been taught for centuries to glory in weakness, in poverty, and in idleness. During the past centuries, the pendulum of thought has swung to the extreme of emphasizing spiritual welfare to the utter neglect of physical welfare. Now the swing of the pendulum is to the opposite extreme. And reformers are becoming wild in their enthusiastic desire to bring about changes and to make regulations for the betterment of the physical status of humanity.

Man is a twofold being. And the New Commandment teaches that each side of his nature must receive equal attention. Each is equally important with the other. We must teach the doctrine of manhood; but, in so doing, we must not forget the doctrine of Godhood. He who aims at manhood's true estate without the ideal of Godhood will become simply a healthy animal. He may, indeed, be far worse than the animal in the field; for his shrewd brain is able to think of acts of which the animal in its natural state would not be capable.

It is generally admitted that the human race, except where civilization has not yet penetrated, in many respects is fast degenerating. So nearly universal is this that men seldom even so much as think of it. If the race is to continue, a halt must be called in this degenerating process. Degeneracy cannot be checked by passing laws concerning eugenics and sexual hygiene, for the reason that the conditions aimed at by teaching eugenics are effects and not causes. To suppress an effect is not to cure a cause. It is like damming up a stream that is continually accumulating. The original outlet may be stopped; but there will result a new outlet, and the new is worse than the old.

In order to remedy race degeneracy, we must go to the root of the difficulty. The New Commandment maintains that the root of the trouble is to be found in an erroneous view of life, an erroneous philosophy and religion, erroneous standards and ideals.

Show man that life is desirable, that, unless he lives on earth and fulfils his duty without grumbling and without complaint, there can be no future happiness and peace for him. Show him as a fundamental fact that, as is the body, so will be the soul, that it is impossible for a strong well-developed soul to abide in a body that is poisoned continually by disease and corrupt habits. Show him that his duty on earth is to be a creator, to work, to accumulate in a natural manner, and to enjoy the fruits of his labor.

Show him that labor, instead of being a shame, is actually for the glorification of the soul. Labor gives health and strength to the body, and keeps the mind occupied and free from morbidity. Convince man that he has a right to health, joy, and happiness. Let him see that denial of health, joy, and happiness is not an indication of soul supremacy, that it is rather a sign of weakness of soul and loss of manhood, and speaks not of kinship with the Father.

First and foremost in the needs of humanity is to have health laws incorporated into its religion. This is a fundamental need; and, unless it is done, the race will continue to decline. Without physical health and vigor there cannot be the highest degree of spirituality. A strong physical foundation is necessary to the attainment of absolute Sonship with the Father. Sonship can only be in accord with the degree of manhood. Unless it is generally recognized that health is a condition of true spirituality and that the health code is on a par with the moral and ethical code, the race cannot attain the ideal of full manhood. Men must recognize that perfection of body, which is the temple of the living God, is of equal importance with perfection of soul. Health and strength of body gives a place to man that is very necessary for the highest degree of Soul Illumination.

Our religion must teach that manliness and manly powers are the means of physical regeneration. Our religion must make clear as a fundamental basis the principle that welfare of body is not antagonistic to welfare of soul. Sad indeed, to think that countless millions have neglected the physical being and its powers so that there has resulted in the race a general decline.

These points in particular, the New Commandmnt teaches. It does not, however, stop with health laws, but includes as laws of life all things that enable man to be at his best both in respect to the physical being and in respect to the soul. Human nature is the foundation of human acts. As such, it is in no wise evil nor destructlve to the soul. But the mind of man should be so normal and so healthy as to be able to recognize the difference between a desire that is good and constructive and one that

is harmful and destructive. The mind should be so healthful as not to be a slave to those desires which can injure
either body or soul.

It is to be greatly regretted that degeneracy is resulting from the erroneous philosophy of life which has
held sway in the minds of the people. Religion has been
made a thing apart from other interests. We have been
taught that the soul is all that counts. And men have
laughed at the idea that one's mode of living and one's
habits and one's work have anything to do with religion
or with the religious life. But the world is fast awakening to different ideas. We are beginning to realize that
this earth life is a school and a training, that care of the
body is as important as care of the soul, and that the labor
of man is as truly a part of religious life as is development of soul. Advance is being made in the right direction. The doctrine of manhood and strength is fast taking
hold of the minds of men. A religion that honors the
body equally with the soul, a religion that guides and con-
trols instinct rather than suppresses it, is absorbing the
interest of thoughtful men. Race betterment is a laudable work; but race betterment can never be brought
about through suppression of desire, nor through ignoring
the value of physical perfection.

Desire for physical perfection is no indication that
man worships the flesh. It is rather an indication that he
desires to become all that he should be. Desire for earthly
possession is by no means an indication that man desires
not Illumination of Soul. It rather indicates a desire to
have that which belongs to him in order to make the most
of life. Desire for strength and power need not indicate
that man would use his strength in forcing the weak to
obey his commands. Desire for strength and power is a
desire to honor God in whose image man is created. Desire to perform useful labor in no wise signifies lack of cul-

ture. It is rather the desire to be a continual creator like the Father. All these things are part of the true man. These desires should be a part of the soul. They should be a part of the religion of the people.

Which is it to be? A religion with manhood as its foundation, teaching progressive growth of both body and soul? Or is it to be a religion of negativeness and decline and degeneracy? Which is it to be?

Force and compulsion cannot bring about gradual development of manhood. Compulsion accomplishes nothing. The race must be educated to higher ideals and standards. The ideal that manhood, strength, and possession, joy, happiness, and a Godly life are desirable must be instilled into the individual mind, and, ultimately, into the race mind. A strong and mighty desire must be created for these very things. Nothing can be done for self-betterment or for race betterment until a strong desire for betterment is created. Let this desire be deeply grounded and rooted in the life of the race. Let it become the foundation upon which our children build their lives; and, within three generations, there will be a race of men such as the world has never seen.

The following principles must be instilled into the minds of men:

In order that man may become the son of God, in order that he may be Godlike, he must round out his true nature. He must become, first of all, MAN, in the true sense of the word. Manhood must be accompanied and followed by the use of his powers in working, in creating, in accomplishing. He must truly act like a prototype of the All Father, the Creator of all things. The life that man lives here on earth is the life that must be taken up again on the next plane, when the soul picks up the thread of being after having thrown off the body. The next life is but a continuation of the present.

When these ideals have become established in the hearts of men, it will be safe to teach mankind eugenics and sexual hygiene. For, then, these sacred sciences will act as an incentive to the true and holy life; whereas, under present standards, they would act as a means of repressing natural instincts, only to create new and worse channels of satisfaction.

CHAPTER EIGHTEEN

"Your Own Will Come to You"—if You Work for It.

"Your own" indicates possession. There is but one source of power. For the individual, that source begins and ends in possession. This being a fundamental truth, it follows that, in order to possess power, it is necessary to come into connection with the source of power; and all possession must be through right methods and principles if it is to be lasting.

In order to possess "your own"—the opportunities and the power that belong to the normal man—it is necessary to obtain health. This is not an easy matter if one has lived a life that was fundamentally wrong, a life that was negative in all its features; for, the desires and the thoughts being negative, the whole being is held in bondage. The philosophy of the weak and diseased man is always wrong. This is a fundamental proposition. That his philosophy is wrong is shown in the fact of his having poor health. Fundamentally, one's philosophy of life is responsible for one's state of health. As a man's philosophy, so is he—that is, as is his real belief, not the philosophy that he professes before men and claims to represent, but that which he believes within his heart of hearts. And, mind you, the vast multitudes believe something, way down within themselves, of which they are not aware; and it is this inner belief which is the essential factor of their life.

The average man may claim to have no religion. Apparently, his claim is true. Yet deep down within himself he is bound as with cables of steel to the religious philosophy of his progenitors. And the philosophy to which he is bound is of the negative type, claiming that the body of man is his enemy, and that, in order to kill this enemy and its desires, it is best to make a slave of the body and to ignore its interests, that the body, existing at best for only a short time, is of little worth, and that the weaker the body and the more racked with pain, the greater is the soul. The man is scarcely conscious of believing these things. He makes no claim to believe them. Apparently, he does not believe them. Yet those ideas are born with him. They are the very foundation of his existence. And he proves it, proves it daily, not only in the results of his life, but in the manner of his living. In order to gain possession of "his own," the true, normal, natural man, first of all, pays strict attention to health and strength. To do 'this demands normal, natural living. It demands carefulness in regard to the habits of daily life. It demands something more than the routine of rising in the morning, eating breakfast, going to work, eating lunch, going to work again, eating dinner, smoking, or going to a place where idle gossip or play is the rule. Such a routine is not the natural life. It is not the life intended by the All Father. It is not the life that makes a man strong and efficient and Godlike. Though in business the man who lives such a life may be what some call "positive," though he may be feeling less toward his fellow men, toward women and children, and may exploit them at every opportunity, nevertheless, his is a negative life. He knows not what good health is. He knows not happiness. He knows nothing of joy or peace of mind.

The true life of man is a double life—the life of the material and the life of the soul. To such a man, existence means more than eating, sleeping, working. To him, it means *living*, and living is a fine art.

First of all, the man who is zealous in securing possession of "his own" adopts a scientific or systematic mode of living. Each day has its round of observances which serve as the outline or skeleton to be filled in and rounded out by duties and pleasures more or less flexible. The morning bath is indispensable, in order to free the body from the poisons that accumulate during the night. If the body is not thus cleansed, these poisons are re-absorbed by the system. The bath must be followed or accompanied by breahing exercises which free the internal body of the poisons therein. This is all-important; for upon the cleanliness of the lungs depend the strength and the power of the material being. A third exercise equally important with physical cleanliness furnishes food and stimulus and freedom for the soul—a silent individual service to God, which should take the form of prayer or a Sacred Mantram held in the heart. This draws the soul near to God, frees the mind and heart of negative conditions, and stimulates mind and heart for the duties of the day.

_The complete life—the life that causes "its own" to come to it—recognizes both body and soul, and considers each equally important with the other. Such a life will eventually realize the highest degree of success. For the service of the soul to its Maker, no church is really necessary; for it is in the privacy of the room, in the privacy of the heart, that true service takes place. The time is not far distant when every man, the head of every family, will have a private room in his own house, to be used as a temple of prayer and worship for himself and his household.

Following these three services, which aim at physical and spiritual cleanliness, man is ready to minister to the demands of the appetite. This should be with food fit for the gods, simple, clean, wholesome,—food that supplies nourishment and strength as well as satisfies the taste.

Nor should one turn immediately from the breakfast

table to business duties and cares. A walk in the open air with deep breathing will charge the blood with vivifying qualities, which are necessary to fit one for the day's labor. The labor of the forenoon, whether physical or menial, should be thought of as wholesome and, in every respect, beneficial to one's welfare. Labor is a glory to mind, heart, and soul, as well as a stimulus to bodily health.

As the breakfast, so should be the lunch, chosen not only to satisfy the taste, but to satisfy the real needs of body, mind, and soul. Then is man ready for further labor. Labor being finished for the day, he should see to it that he and his family enjoy some wholesome exercise, after which follows the evening meal. Then comes recreation and pleasure, whatever will cheer the heart and the soul of himself and of those dependent on him.

It is to be hoped that the time is not far distant when the ancient rule will be followed, when the twenty-four inch gauge will be divided ino three parts and will be strictly adhered to, one part for labor, one part for rest, one part for recreation. No man should be forced to work more than one third of the day. No one, except under special circumstances, needs more rest than one third of the day. He does, however, need that much and should see to it that he has opportunity for that amount of rest. Every individual—man, woman, and child—requires the other third for the needs of the spiritual being and for recreation and pleasure. This ancient guage of life is the normal, natural division of time for man.

While man is on the earth it is necessary for him to have regard for the body as the dwelling place of mind and soul. The mind should be clear and rational in its operations. The soul should be as free as possible from taint and blemish and from the poison of negative thought conditions. Unless the body is healthy and strong and normal, the individual is more or less handicapped in every direction. No man can reach the highest degree of success, who neglects the body. It is for this reason that he who aims at true success must give first attention to physical strength and vigor. It is for this reason that he who aims at Soul Illumination and Sonship with God must give first attention to physical needs. The body is the foundation of the soul, and the soul cannot be at its best unless the body is at its best. A strong, healthy body makes it easy for the mind to be clear and to think consecutively and logically. Health of body makes it easy to think constructive thoughts, to THINK, and then to BUILD, success.

The possibilities of success are greater than they have ever been in the history of the world. Everywhere, there is a demand for men. But they must be *men* in the true sense of the word, men of strength and not weaklings, men whose minds are free from malice, hate, and destructive thoughts. They must be men whose minds are clear, men who recognize the fundamental fact that if they do not succeed it is not because some one is holding them back, not because some one has power over them, but simply because they are slaves to weakness, to misconceptions, slaves to the belief that others are holding them back and that others are interfering with their desiny.

Men must gain freedom from the idea that a few men control the world. They must recognize that health, power, strength, possession, are the inheritance of all men, and that if they do not possess these things it is because they do not take advantage of the opportunities that are held before them continually.

Note the difference between two men. Here is one who is weak and far from perfect in health, but his mind is filled with theories. He may have an understanding of fundamental laws, but he does not make use of them. This man is well educated; nevertheless, when it comes to the race of life and the survival of the fittest, he is sadly handicapped. Here is another man who may not have the education, but has physical strength and endurance and a great fund of wholesome thought and courage. He is able to step in and do things. He knows not fear. Nor does he shrink from responsibility. In the race of life, this man stands a better chance than the former.

The race of life is to the strong. It is to those who, being normal, see with clear vision. It is to them because they have the courage and the power, because they are in possession of that which helps them to pass others with a bound.

But because man is weak is no reason he should remain weak. It is his duty, aye, his privilege, to leave weakness behind, and to gain strength, health, and courage, step by step, until perfection is his. At first, this requires great courage. All new beginnings require courage. As one takes the first step in the right direction and refuses to turn back, he receives strength and courage for the next step. And, if he continues to refuse a backward step, the goal eventually will be health, strength, and power.

In the struggle for possession of "his own"—be it what it may, whether possession of health and strength, happiness, love, peace, or material treasures—there is always the enemy to be met. This enemy is fear. No sooner is man ready to leave the old way for the new than fear steps in and bids him halt.

Fear reasons thus: 'To give up the old is to reap condemnation. The old, the negative is right. To seek bodily strength and earthly treasures is to lose the soul and to miss the reward. Possession is wrong. It is better to be a slave, slave to want, to disease, to weakness, to poverty, to the exploitation of others; for this is to gain the kingdom of heaven—after death.'

This is the old enemy to possession, the enemy that

has held in bondage vast multitudes for centuries. The enemy, fear, includes ignorance, bigotry, and the desire to do nothing. On account of obedience to this cruel enemy, we have the woe and the misery that are everywhere apparent: on the one side, the vast multitudes, which are exploited by the few; on the other, the few who exploit men, women, and children—and all for what reason? Simply because men—or beings in the form of men—have listened to the old destructive philosophy, which has taught man that, in slavery, there is salvation of soul, and that slavery is the gateway to the kingdom of heaven—after death.

Free yourself from these shackles. Look life in the face. Look at it unflinchingly. Defy the evil in it. Follow the right. Follow the path to strength, to possession, to happiness, to peace and joy. Follow the path to manhood, no matter what the old tempter within yourself may say. Follow the path to manhood though the enemy may try to convince you that the path will lead to destruction. Once you take a determined start in the path of manhood toward Godhood, you will gain strength, you will see with clear eyes, you will realize that it is good to live, and that life is, in every respect, desirable, that honest possessions bring joy, power, influence, which may be used in the cause of right..

One of the most formidable of the negative principles is this: "Your own will come to you." One of the most inviting of the positive principles is this: "Your own will come to you if you work for it."

Without doubt, the doctrine that your own will come to you has been the cause of more failures, more suffering, than all others. For it puts a premium on doing nothing. It exalts folding one's hands and waiting, believing that what is to be will be, that if we are to have something we will get it, either with effort or without effort, here being no difference whether we make effort or not.

Truly "our own"—that which we deserve—will come to us. And if we live a negative life, idle and listless and effortless, nothing is due us, and that very thing—nothing —will be sure to come to us. Man receives what he earns. If he takes that which he does not earn, it will be snatched from him through the power of the immutable law of justice.

Man is placed on the earth with a mission. He has been given the right and the privilege of choice. Furthermore, *he has been given the power to get what he chooses.* But the stipulation is made by the law, that whatever he chooses will not come unless he makes the effort to get it. *If he makes the effort, fearing nothing, dauntless and full of courage, allowing nothing to turn him aside, waiting not for better opportunities or for a more favorable time, he will get what he wants. "His own," his cherisheed ambition, will be his.*

Failure to possess "one's own," one's desired treasure, is due either to fear or to a false philosophy. Fear presents itself in many shades and degrees—fear of failing, fear of being wrong, fear of this and that. A false philosophy teaches man that if he is to have a thing he will get it, come what may; and the result is, he makes no effort.

The true man brushes aside both fear and a false philosophy of life. He knows that nothing will come to him unless he earns it, unless he puts forth effort. He knows that he is co-creator with God. He knows that if he wants a thing he must get it, that God gives man nothing, but that man must take what he wants and that if he would keep what he takes he must get it justly.

To be interested in something is not enough. It is absolutely necessary for our interest to be so intense that we shall not give up until we attain our wish, no matter what may come. Neither poverty nor fear will prevent us from attaining it. The desire to do is the power to do, but the WILL to do must be present also.

Your own will come to you when you want it badly enough to be willing to work for it. Your own will come to you when you are willing to *demand* it, to work and to demand until you have it. Wishing is by no means enough.

These are fundamental laws. That they are absolute is amply proved by the great successes in life. Men born in poverty have achieved. A desire to accomplish, a willingness to work, to slave, if necessary, and an indomitable will to surmount all obstacles, have made successes of men who had apparently little chance in life.

It is by surmounting difficulties and obstacles that man gains strength. Every barrier overcome means power. All barriers, all obstacles, give way when man says, "I will." He who does not give up, not even if death itself appears, will overcome even death in his dauntless search for the thing he desires.

The New Commandment advocates a natural, normal life, a life that leads to manhood's true estate. It advocates that manhood is necessary to the attainment of Godhood. It teaches that soul growth, an active desire for Soul Illumination, and an effort to attain this, is necessary in order to reach Illumination of Soul, and that Manhood must go hand in hand with Soulhood and Godhood.

OTHER IMPORTANT BOOKS

ALL THESE ARE TEMPLE OF ILLUMINATI PUB-
LICATIONS

THE SON OF GOD.

Called the Mystical Teachings of the Masters. This
book gives a summarization of the fundamental principles of the Christic Interpretation and the characteristics of the Christic Law, as advocated by the
Temples of the Illuminati and Illumination. The
teachings of the Essenes under whom Jesus studied,
etc. Price in cloth, 50 cents; in paper covers, 25
cents.

CHRISTHOOD AND ADEPTSHIP.

Christic power can be awakened only though obedience to the Divine Law. When we obey the Divine
Law, then will the Christ Child be born within us; and,
if we continue in the Way, this child grows to manhood and enters into power. This is one of the first
text-books of the Christic Interpretation series.
Bound in beautiful cloth, side stamp in gold, 75 cents.

SOUL SCIENCE AND IMMORTALITY.

The standard text-book of the Illuminati. It is universally admitted among scholars that we are on the
Threshold of a new Dispensation. This means that
we are expecting a new Law that shall govern all

things. To state this more correctly, we are expecting a New Interpretation of the old Law, an Interpretation that is at once practical and mystical.
This book gives such an Interpretation. More than
200 pages, beautifully bound in cloth, side and back
stamped in gold. Price $1.50.

THE MYSTICAL INTERPRETATION OF ST. JOHN

This is a complete and exhaustive Mystical Interpretation of the Gospel of St. John, so well called
the Philosopher of Love. Contains 53 Chapters or
Lessons, beautifully bound in cloth, side and back
stamped in gold. Price $1.25.

THE CHRISTIC INTERPRETATION OF ST. MAT-THEW.

This is a complete Interpretation of the Gospel of
St. Matthew. Contains 73 lessons, 265 pages. It is
the most complete book of its kind. Beautifully
bound in cloth, side and back stamped in gold. Price
$1.25.

CHRISTISIS.

The standard text-book on Higher Soul Culture.
Students who have this book say that it is the best,
clearest, and most practical book that they have been
able to find. It is beautifully bound in imitation
leather, side and back stamped in gold. Price, $5.00.

Any of these books will be forwarded on receipt of
remittance. Catalog giving exhaustive description of the
contents of these books will be mailed with pleasure.

The Philosophical Publishing Co.,
Allentown, Pa.